ESCAPING THE ALLURE OF THE GAME
'MARRIED TO THE GAME'

Shaunta Kenerly

KENERLY PRESENTS PUBLICATION

ISBN-13:
978-0692572825

ISBN-10:
0692572821

Graphic Art:

Shots By Vegas Photography @fiyahmagazine
fiyahmagllc@gmail.com

Cover Model:

England Payne @fiyah_beautifulgem
dawnjo50@yahoo.com

shauntakenerlypresents@gmail.com

Printed in the United States of America

Chapter 1

The sun peaked through my cell window waking me up. I made my bed military style and slid on my ugly brown flip flops. I slid over to the toilet and pissed for what seemed forever. My cell mate rolled over in his bed moaning but he knew not to say a word or I word have made him touch everything in here. I rushed to brush my teeth because I knew that at any moment the guard on duty would be unlocking the doors for breakfast chow. The breakfast was always the same bullshit, a handful of dried generic cereal, a school sized milk, and a piece of stale ass bread. Even if I asked for water it would only be enough to give to a little kid. I never understood why they gave us the same shit but I was hoping that I would only wake up to this shit a few more times.

The media tried to make my case a high profile case due to what Christian did and the feds being all over it. They heard all of the terrible stories my crew was accused of since we were kids and they were glad we were off the street. The feds wanted to make me an example to all of the dealers in the Mid-West. My case was on the internet, newspapers, and they even had a television show saying that we were captured. Every time I went to court, the front of the federal building would be packed full of reporters as far as Detroit and Louisville, Kentucky. My lawyer asked for the location be moved from Dayton to Columbus but Magistrate Thomas Anderson said "no."

That was just the beginning of my problems with the media.

I had a problem with them harassing my aunt and my wife at their homes. They were in front of our house just waiting for the opportunity to get an interview with Diana alone. They thought my woman would have given them some insight on my case. They must be crazy. The media even followed Diana to her mother's house one time after leaving court. Diana was fed up with their tactics and called the police. That was the only time they did something useful for my family. My aunt cursed they ass out so violently that they would just end up leaving. It took three different news stations to get the point of not to bother her until she allowed them to come in her house one day. She left them alone in her living room while she went to her room. My aunt came out with a shotgun, ready to answer any stupid ass question that they had for her nephew. Although she was small and probably only weighed about 130 pounds, they weren't about to try her. My lawyer said he would make a few calls and he did. The media stopped hounding my family but they didn't stop hounding me. I wondered where were they when my brother got killed in broad daylight. As usual the media only wanted to highlight negativity in the hood. They never came around when I gave out food each Thanks Giving to the homeless. The fact that my brother was gunned down by the police didn't matter. He was a known affiliate of "The 75 Boyz." The media were happy to get another drug dealer and reported gang member off the streets one way or another.

My lawyer had been visiting me daily since the trial was on the horizon. I have been down here in the county jail held with a two million dollar bond over a year now. The lawyer had tried to get my bail lowered stating that my family needed me but the judge considered me a flight risk. He was absolutely right. I would have got the fuck out of here not looking back at all. I just hoped to get the bail down to five hundred thousand then I could get my black ass out of this dirty ass place.

After our small confrontation, my lawyer had gotten his shit all of the way together. He wasn't taking me for a dummy or a fool that would take what these wake ass prosecutors was offering. I believed that I could beat the case if they would present their evidence against me. Shit I was more interested with finding out who was their star witness to testify against me. I was still in disbelief that one of my childhood friends would snitch on me. I planned on going to trial just to meet this rat face to face. Finding out was worth the wait. Today the wait was over.

I climbed out of the bed and looked out of the small rectangular shaped glass on my door. The porters walked out of their cells to help with serving us inmates. Officer Walter Monroe was on duty. He and I went way back. I had been knowing him and his father since I was sixteen years old. Monroe's father used to be a cop and he ran a program in our neighborhood to keep kids away from drugs and gangs. I guess that shit didn't work for me and my crew.

Walter was running in the streets on the east side at the time being a spoiled brat looking for attention or some shit. Until a year or two later he became a young junkie. Walter did anything he could to get his next high. He broke in cars, broke in houses, sold fake dope, and I even caught him sucking dick just to get high. He was in the dope spot begging this old head drug dealer for a front but the old head wasn't budging. Walter offered everything he thought he could steal but the old head had a crazy look in his eye. The old head rushed to bag up my little ounce and told me to get the fuck out of the room. I didn't want to question what was going because I knew the old head had slipped up and gave me about an extra quarter and I was going to ball with it. Before I could take one step out of the door, I looked over my shoulder and Walter was on his knees unzipping the man. I stood shocked until Walter grabbed the man's shaft and put it in his mouth.

I often ran into Walter over there with him spending nights and wearing the same shit on for days at a time. He tried to sell me stolen items but I would remind him that I was in the business to make money not to spend it on some hot shit. After while he wouldn't even give me eye contact or speak to me. I assumed he felt embarrassed. He became a crack house bitch.

The old head spot started to become hot with Walter selling stolen shit, fiends coming in and out, and old head started having hoes fucking there John's in a spare room. I had to quit fucking with him and only fuck with my homie Keith because I wasn't going to get caught up in the bullshit. The cops soon after raided the spot. When his father's fellow cops found him in the crack-house they didn't run him in, instead they took him home to his dad. Mr. Monroe didn't want his junkie son to destroy his name and legacy so he quickly put him in a rehab to get him all of the way together. That only took three tries and thousands of dollars.

When Officer Monroe ran our block, I made sure that he knew that I needed to handle business. That meant a lot of time outside of my cell to ride on the phone and stay up on my ESPN. Sometimes I would change to the local news to see if anyone else that I knew was being brought in or killed in the streets. I was never surprised by our local news. Our murder rate continued to rise and junkies were dying left and right off of the brown dope that they were shooting into their veins. Monroe knew not to play that tough guy shit with me because I would exploit his bitch ass in a minute and get him touched in the streets. Monroe would wait until everyone including the porters would get back in their cell to allow me out. He would only ask that I pretend like I am cleaning up for a while before I got on the phone. I played along.

Like clockwork my door buzzed open after everyone went back to bed. I nodded my head at him saying thanks and grabbed a rag and spray bottle. I wiped down a few tables and then made my way to the phone. I heard Monroe giggling at me but I ignored him and dialed up my wife.

"Good morning love," I said softly using my bedroom voice.

"Hey you," Diana responded sounding excited to hear my voice.

"Are you ready for today?" I asked.

"Yes I am but your son is getting on my last nerve," Diana said smacking her lips.

"What's the problem?" I wondered what he could be up to this damn early in the morning.

"He refuses to put his shoes on. I don't have time to mess with him this morning," Diana answered.

"He's still sleepy that's all," I countered defending my little man.

"Maybe. Rico! Your daddy is on the phone."

"Hi daddy!" Rico said with excitement.

"What's up son? You know daddy loves you right?"

"Yeah," Rico said giggling.

"Well daddy needs you to put your shoes on so you can go over your aunt's house. Can you do that for me?"

"Yeah," Rico answered.

Diana got back on the phone, "What did you tell him? Because he took off to his room."

"I just asked him to put his shoes on," I responded.

"I wish you were here to deal with him all of the time he acts like that," she said sadly.

"I will be very soon. I think I got this case beat."

"Have you talked to your lawyer lately?" Diana questions knowingly.

"Yes, of course. He will meet me over in the courtroom. The guards should be coming up to get me soon."

"Well baby, I will let you go. I still have to drop Rico off but I will be there on time."

"I'll see you soon then baby."

"I hope I get to have you really soon. It hasn't been the same without you," Diana countered.

"I'm coming home baby best believe it!" I said trying to assure her.

"I hope so. I am ready for us to enjoy our honeymoon."

"We will, and many more nights of love making."

"Boy don't get me started and I can't do anything."

"Go ahead and play with it for me," I said whispering into the phone.

"No not right now," she laughed.

"Just a few more days and we are going to be at it like wild animals I promise!" I raised my voice imagining us having sex.

"Reese, I hear you talking but I bet I will be the one all over you. I can't wait to ride that dick. You can do whatever you want."

"That's what I like to hear," I responded noticing my manhood growing strong with the thought.

You have one minute left for this call. The recording interrupts.

"Well babe, I'll see you later. Love you."

"Damn just when it was getting good!" I shout into the phone.

Diana laughs.

"Love you to," I said ending the call.

I hung the phone up and went back to playing things off. I sprayed the rag and wiped down the phones. Although I was pretending to be a porter, I was honestly glad to wipe down the phones. The jail houses all types of folks from the drug dealers, robbers, dead beat dads, the crazies, traffic violators, and a lot of homeless people. Without any way of truly knowing what someone has, it's good to be doing my part with killing some of these germs. I wasn't trying to get sick with anything.

While cleaning the phones, my mind wasn't set for the start of my trial but on the thought of holding Diana in my arms. I wanted her bad. The visits between glass drove me crazy. She didn't have to say anything sexual to me and my manhood would be standing at attention. Maybe it was her presence. Maybe it was how full her luscious lips are. I wanted to suck the lip-gloss off her lips through the glass. Every time she'd visited me I imagined just having her physically.

"Maurice!" Officer Monroe shouted trying to sound tough.

"Yo!"

"You have mail!" he answered with a grin.

I sat down the rag and spray bottle and rushed over to the desk. Monroe stuffed the letter back into the envelope and handed it over. I grabbed the letter and walked over to the stainless steel table to read what's inside. I flipped the envelope over and I noticed that the letter is from Sky.

I smiled.

Sky was the last person that I had sex with. As hard as it was to say that but it was the truth. Diana and I had planned to make love every day on our honeymoon but the feds busted into our wedding ceremony ruining our lives.

I met Sky and two of her friends at my bachelor's party. It was a good night. They had put on a show for me at the party which left me dying to find out if Sky was just a good dancer or a good fuck. B said a few words to the ladies and the next thing I knew they were walking out from the dressing room with their bags. They decided to meet me back in my hotel room and gave me a party that I would always remember.

Sky was really trying to be my down ass side chic. She was more than willing to accept her place and respect my woman. Since I had been in here she had visited me multiple times, sent me a gang of letters and had even collected some money from some of my young homies to keep Diana straight. I often sat in my cell contemplating the idea of having her as my side chic. To me Sky was everything for me that Diana wasn't. The job couldn't be filled by a more suitable person.

I could smell the scent of the letter seeping through the envelope. All of her letters smelt the same. The wonderful scent of Kim K's perfume. Sky wanted to remind me of her scent from the night she had her pussy all in my face. I couldn't resist from smiling each time I saw a letter with her name on it.

Today was special. Not only was she writing me a nasty ass letter with promises of another night of hot sex but she'd included some pictures. Sky sent me three photos of her in lingerie and the forth with her in the bathroom with just a towel on.

Right on time. I said to myself.

I put away the cleaning supplies and rushed for my cell. I almost fell speed walking around the tables so fast. I grabbed my towel, fresh draws, washcloth, soap, and my favorite picture of her. I speed walked again to the showers up on the second range for more privacy.

Inside of the shower, I'd lathered my hands up causing the soap to foam. I sit Sky's picture behind the soap dish. I played back the night in my hotel room. I imagined myself hitting her from the back. I remember holding her hips firmly as I drove deep inside her. I mold my hand to fit perfectly around my shaft. With my eyes closed tightly, I began to stroke myself slowly. With each stroke I imagined I was going deeper inside of her. Faster I stoked imagining her ass bouncing off of my thighs. I changed speed, and remembered slow stroking her as Sky laid on her back eating her friend Therapy. Suddenly I felt my shaft harden ready to explode. I picture her breasts bouncing with each stoke.

"Awwww!" I grunt having an orgasm.

I squirted a heavy load onto the drain. Some of the nut didn't make it down the drain so I scoot it with my flipper. After getting rid of the evidence, I allowed the water to rinse off the soap from my penis. My penis has a burning sensation to it. I must have jacked off so hard that I got some soap into my penis. I continued to wash up until I heard Officer Monroe making his rounds on the tier. All of the guards can be heard from far away by the unique sounds of their boots and keys.

Monroe stopped in front of my shower door, "Whenever you're done pulling on your little chicken neck, you should get out. They just called up saying that they were about to come and get you for a lawyer visit."

"Thanks man," I said quickly drying off.

I rushed back to my cell and hurried to throw on my county blues. I sat on the edge of my bed anticipating the buzz on the door again.

Chapter 2

Two hours later...

Buzz!

"Step out with your blues on and shut the door behind you," Officer Monroe ordered over the speaker in my room. He amused me trying to sound tough.

I slipped back on my flip flops and stepped out the door. Two guards greeted me outside of the door. One swung the hand cuffs and ankle cuffs like he was anticipating to put them on me. The jail had to send the biggest guards up here. They asked me to put my arms out and then they had slapped the cuffs on. After securing the handcuffs, they told me to turn around and raise on leg at a time. I made sure that I wore two pair of socks to keep the cuffs from cutting up my skin.

Soon as we get off of the elevator, four agents assist the guards with the efforts. I was thinking to myself that they must think that I will try to run or I must have a team ready to come into the courtroom on some movie shit. There wasn't anybody dumb enough to do a suicide trip nor was I going to try to run. This was just to make me look worst for the media I assumed.

The county guards stood outside of a holding cell while I was being watched by the four feds while I got dressed. Diana brought my suit that I wore when the crew and I had our grand opening for the club. The suit alone brought back a lot of memories. All of us getting money and three of us were living. White Boy, Amad, and Christian now gone. Now I am faced with this bullshit all alone.

B and Tone were co-defendants while Mar and I were being charge with other charges. Mar had some weapon charges to add to his long list of charges. Our lawyers thought it was best to be separate from the rest of the crew. My lawyer assured me that I had a better chance of getting off without the whole crew especially without knowing what all the evidence the DEA had on us. I agreed. I just prayed every night that God would have favor on us even the so called friend whom was running his mouth.

Diana told me that B coped out to 5 years about a week ago. Mar took 7 years and Tone took 5 years probation due to the fact he hadn't ever been in any trouble. Shit, Tone was in just the same amount of shit as the rest of us. She said Tone was on house-arrest until he officially was sentenced. The only one who just jumped off the porch into the game was Christian. But shit, if he were here he would be sitting right next to me dealing with this shit. That wasn't the life I had in mind for my brother.

I was being escorted by four agents and two county deputy guards to the courtroom. They couldn't have made the handcuffs any tighter around my wrists. I continued to wiggle my fingers enable to keep the blood circulating. I was bouncing off of the guards like a bowling ball. The two county guards pulled on my arms forcefully until I reached a big mahogany door. It read Court Room 2C Magistrate

Thomas Anderson. Pictures of current and old judges hung on the hall walls with their fake ass smiles. Various reporters voices echoed through the halls before I was pushed into the courtroom. I laughed as I saw them trying to rush in my direction.

Finally I saw my lawyer sitting with his expensive Italian suit and Steve Harvey haircut along with two other lawyers on his staff. I stood next to my lawyer and lifted my hands to shake his. My lawyer looked over my shoulder and directly at the deputies. With his eyes he'd asked them to uncuff me. Without any rebuttal one of the deputies took out his keys and released me. I stared them all down until they walked away.

I was sitting next to my lawyer waiting for the judge to enter the court room. My eyes searched the room for Diana, and within a few seconds I found her sitting in the back of the courtroom. She sat alone with a tan floppy hat on her head looking like a young Mary J. I hate myself for putting her through this shit.

Suddenly my lawyer stood up and walked across from us. My eyes followed him not knowing who he was talking to. Then I notice two people that I hate most in this world, Agent Rivera and Agent Candace Jackson.

Candace kept her focus off of me and onto the bench where the judge sat. But jerk ass Agent Rivera stared me down like I was a bitch. I returned his gesture with a mean-mug facial expression. He smiled at me with this strange look on his face like he hated my guts. Fuck him, I said to myself.

My lawyer walked back to us after his brief conversation with the other men. "He wants to play hard ball," he said walking around me making sure he didn't step on my feet. My lawyer fixed his suit and took a drink of water and what it seemed like he was getting into a zone. I nodded my head excited myself.

I could only imagine what he and the prosecutors discussed. I knew that I wasn't going to take the 15 years that they'd offered at first. My son would be a grown ass man when I got out. My lawyer and his team also said that the deal was nuts. When my lawyer came in with the offer I quickly said "no deal" like I was on the old game show. I wanted to see their evidence and this fucking rat.

The judge entered the court room and we all stood to our feet. He took his seat and surveyed the room. Not long after he collected some paperwork from the bailiff he opened up with a joke. The courtroom busted out laughing but I wasn't in a laughing mood. I looked back and Diana wasn't laughing either. When the courtroom settled down, he opened up with an honest question for my lawyer. He said that he was aware of the offer the federal prosecutors offered and wanted to make sure that I was sure about my decision. My lawyers stated that I was fully aware of my choice and wanted to continue with the trial.

The prosecutor opened statements had me itching to get out of my seat and whoop his ass. He talked about my crew like we were the Russian mob. He claimed that we had our neighborhood residents held captive. Like they were prisoners in their own home. Shit we feed the streets literally. We did a lot for the kids and helped out junkies with their fixes.

The first person to take the stage was my store manager Dennls. The prosecutor asked Dennls If I was In the courtroom and he pointed straight at me. He avoided eye contact while he was asked by the prosecutor if he'd ever noticed any drug activity in the shop. He testified that he hasn't ever seen with his eyes of anything but had heard that I was an ex-drug dealer. Dennis testified that I was always respectful and honest. He said he didn't believe it when people would tell him those stories.

After Dennis's testimony, the prosecutor showed pictures of Christian and I meeting outside of the laundromat, pictures that Candace took showing the inside, and pictures of me bringing my bank bag in and out. It was hard to resist from saying something out loud to the prosecutor but I kept my mouth closed. My lawyer leaned over and whispered in my ear that their evidence wasn't sufficient because he didn't prove that I had any dope or used the money for dope.

I sat back in my chair and just watched the lawyer talk shit. I couldn't wait for my lawyer to tear his ass up. I'd fixed my tie and looked over at the jurors. I didn't recognize any of them but a young black dude stood out. His face looked hard and his beard was thick like mine. I noticed he had tattoos on his hands so I'd believed he was from the city.

I continued to observe the courtroom anticipating when would this star witness take the stand. I had been in the courtroom for over an hour. I wondered would Candace take the stand and if she did, I wanted my lawyer to present the video tape of us having sex in the laundromat. I know that Diana would be embarrassed but I had to do what I had to do to get back to her.

The prosecutor requested for Detective Shaw to take the stand. I couldn't wait to see this coward. I was still surprised that he was free after being caught red handed with drugs in his possession. Detective Shaw was sworn in and started to answer questions from the prosecutor. I was amazed by all of the information he had to testify. My lawyer crossed examined Shaw asking him about how he got caught up in the dope game. I checked for any response from the jury and they were appalled. Hearing that a member of the police force was convicted of drug possession hit hard. My lawyer wanted the prosecution to make it clear to everyone that they were using Detective Shaw to testify against me although he had been proven not to be trustworthy. I believed it worked.

The prosecutors were feeling the heat from my lawyer and decided to bring both agents to the stand. Both agents did an excellent job testifying. Of course Agent Rivera made sure he added that my brother and I were the biggest drug dealers that he has ever came across. Candace just answered questions like I was just another dealer. Her answers weren't lies or emphasized to make me look bad. I still wanted my lawyer to add the new evidence of the video tape.

Soon as Candace walked past me to take her seat, the prosecutor talked amongst his assistants and shuffle through some folders.

I turned to look at Candace and whispered to her that I will be out of this bitch today. I just felt that I had this case beat.

This muthafucka was lost. He was trying to find some shit on me. I said to myself with laughter.

The judge cleared his throat, "Councilor are you prepared to present your next witness?"

"Yes judge. He just called my colleague and said he was in the building," the prosecutor defends.

"He..."

The doors suddenly swung opened allowing the chatter from the reporters to enter the courtroom. I turned to look this rat dead in his eyes and to my surprise they did sucker one of my boys on their side. A muthafucka I would have taken a bullet for. A muthafucka I had called my brother. A muthafucka I had brought around my son. A muthafucka I thought I could trust.

Tone.

His ass took a deal alright. I knew that shit sounded too good to be true when Diana told me about it. Especially since they had pictures of B and him working the streets together. Damn, I know B was sick behind this sorry ass muthafucka.

"Your honor, I call Antonio Curtis to the stage," the prosecutor announced after taking a sip of water.

We had been calling Tone by his nickname for so damn long I had almost forgotten his government. Shit after today I was going to forget his bitch ass forever. The bad part about it was that he knew the streets were going to talk and I was going to find out sooner than later. He couldn't ever go back to the hood or be caught anywhere close to the city. I had too much love out there and I feed a lot of young dealer when they were kids. They would be the first to go see him. I hope that the feds had placed him in protective custody because his ass was good as dead.

Tone was sworn in then took his seat.

More guards entered from the back of the courtroom and stood near the jury box.

"Mr. Curtis, can you please state your name and nickname for the court so that we can identify you," the prosecutor requested standing near Tone.

"Yes sir. My name is Antonio Curtis and my nickname is Tone," Tone answered looking like he was about to jump off of a cliff.

"Were you once affiliated with a drug organization in Dayton Ohio called the 75/70 Boys?"

"Yes sir."

"Can you identify the leader of that drug organization in this courtroom today?"

"Yes sir," Tone answered sounding like a good ole boy.

"Can you please point out the person you are testifying is the drug organization's leader," the prosecutor ordered leaning against the bench where the jurors sat.

Tone pointed directly at me. I know he felt the heat coming from my chair. One thing we all supposed to have hatted the most was rats.

"Let the court acknowledge that Mr. Curtis identified the defendant Mr. White," the prosecutor announced with a sneaky looking grin on his face. He walked back over to Tone and proceeded to ask questions.

Tone started from the beginning when we'd first started out selling $10 blunts of weed in our high school bathroom. I remembered that he was the one that got us the sacks from his uncle. We didn't graduate to selling cocaine and heroin until our senior year of high school.

We all decided that it was time to make some real money and with making real money came real problems. We had to take over our neighborhood blocks first. We all put in work putting the tool to our competitors forcing them out the hood. Within three months we had five dope houses and a stash house and we were only eighteen and nineteen years old. We were going through two bricks of coke a week and a half brick of dog food.

Just thinking back, I am still shocked that this bitch ass muthafucka was snitching. All of the dirt he had done and he turned on his homies as soon as it got hot. These muthafucking prosecutors knew that they didn't have anything on me for real until this rat rolled over on me. Getting this case thrown out was out of the question. He was telling a story about us like he had wrote a script for a movie. Shit he was giving the court room too much information.

I continued to sit and listen to him as he dug my ditch for my grave deeper and deeper. My blood boiled through my veins like I was about to explode. This shiestie muthafucka only wanted to make sure he was free from these dirty prosecutors. All we had been through didn't mean shit. Loyalty and honor were just words muthafuckas threw around. Ain't no rules in this game. At the end of the day I could only trust myself.

My lawyer proceeded to ask Tone questions about his role with the crew. Tone tried to play it coy like he was a victim. He testified that he was forced into the game by our society and poverty that he was brought up in. I couldn't help but blurt out a laugh at this crazy ass dude.

I glued my eyes right on his as he left the stand being protected by a federal guard. I noticed him look over at Diana and she just shot back a disgusted look at him as he left the courtroom.

My lawyer knowing that I wanted to bring the tape into play asked the judge for a brief break. The judge asked why and he shocked the crowd with the news that we had additional evidence for the court. The judge asked the prosecutor was he aware of this new evidence and he'd answered no. The courtroom began to chatter. The judge ordered for a thirty minute recess and I was escorted out the courtroom again put back in handcuffs.

My lawyer soon joined me. "Mr. White are you sure that you would like to show this tape to the jury?"

"Yes I do! They will have to meet me in the middle on this deal."

"So do you want me to offer them a deal?" My lawyer asked turning for the door.

"I want us all in here to discuss a deal. I'm not about to allow y'all to decide my life. I will be in control of it."

"I will request for the prosecutors to join us. Give me a moment," my lawyer said walking out the door.

Within minutes, my lawyers and the prosecutors entered the room. A deputy also entered the room and guarded the door. He stood at ease with his arms behind his back and feet spread shoulder length apart.

My lawyers must have already showed the prosecutors the tape because when they had sat down they asked us what did we want. Like a genius, my lawyer asked for my charges to be dropped. I nodded my head yes while I simultaneously searched the room for their reaction. The head prosecutor laughed and slapped his thick folder full of papers on the table.

"This what we have agreed on offering you and this is not up for any debate. If you agree to this deal you can not mention the video tape or Agent Jackson in anything," the prosecutor said.

"What's the deal," I asked sounding nervous. My eyes traveled from their faces to down in my lap.

"We can offer you ten years and a few months," the prosecutor said leaning back in his chair like he was a boss.

"That ain't no muthafucking deal man!" I shouted getting the attention from the guard.

"Calm down Mr. White! I know we can work something out," my lawyer aggressively interjected.

"Mr. White we can easily get you for conspiracy to distribute a controlled substance and maybe even money laundering out of your laundromat," the assistant prosecutor finally spoke up.

"Money laundering? Y'all muthafuckas must really think I am a kingpin or something. I never did anything in my place of business besides fuck the shit out of Agent Jackson. Fuck you mean money laundering?"

"Look, you and I know that from the testimony of Mr. Curtis alone that there isn't any judge that will agree to give you anything less than 12 years after being convicted. I am trying to work with you so that I can go home to my family. I don't want to drag this case out another month or so for nothing. And Mr. White, I know that you don't want to be away from your pretty wife for that long time. Imagine being hundreds of miles away from her, no visits, no kisses, no nothing. Please take the deal and get home to your family," the lead prosecutor said firmly remaining to sit relaxed like this was a walk in the park.

"You know what fuck It. Fuck It!" I barked slamming my fist against the wood table. I felt the handcuffs tighten. The guard took a step closer but the lead prosecutor waved him to stop.

"Mr. White, you don't..."my lawyer spoke up but I quickly cut him off.

"Yes. Yes I do! Sir you are absolutely right. But I do have a few things for my defense. The fact that I am not in any pictures or recordings with anything proven to be drugs, helps me. The fact that your star witness is a snitch that should be in this room with me and is just trying to save himself, helps me. The fact that I have a clear video tape of me smashing your witness, helps me. Don't let my lawyer remind the jury about your agents gunning down my brother. Now I don't have a problem with allowing the jury to decide my fate. I'm sure you feel like this case can go any way and I know with the amount of media on this case you don't want to lose it. So let me tell you the deal I would take."

"I'm listening," the prosecutor said brushing his neatly trimmed beard with his hand.

"I will take six years and the chance at an early release. Also because you'd mentioned the distance between my wife and I, I don't want to be that far away from her."

The prosecutor and his assistant laughs, "That is a hell of a list. Did you just make this list up?"

"I don't see what's so damn funny," I said starring them down. I'd felt my fist ball up ready to go upside one of their heads.

"We can't give you all of that," the assistant prosecutor said.

"Well shit fuck it! I'll see y'all muthafuckas back in the courtroom!" I aggressively said biting down on my bottom lip pissed as fuck.

"Sirs give me another moment to talk to my client," my lawyer said standing to his feet. His eyes where big as hell surprised by my remarks.

"Talk for what? I'm not taking 10, 12, or 15 years! You didn't catch me with shit!" I spat.

I looked over at my lawyer and he'd just stared back not saying a word. I felt cornered. I knew that I played the hand I was dealt.

"Let me discuss the offer with my client," my lawyer interjected.

All of the lawyers got up from their seats and left the room. The lead prosecutor walked out with the same grin on his face he had in the courtroom.

My lawyer waited for everyone to leave the door before he'd spoke, "Reese, you should have allowed me to do my fucking job. I had these muthafuckas where I wanted them. They believed we were going to take it all of the way but with you striking a deal with them they might just try us for real."

"Shit let em," I responded.

"Mr. White, he's right. If you are found guilty, the judge won't be lenient. He will sentence you to the max if not the max. You can get 10 to life."

"What should we do?" I asked feeling my life was now officially in his hands.

"I can get you a good deal. I saw it in his eyes. He don't want to lose this case and I don't either. Honestly Reese, it's too close to call," my lawyer said pulling out a pad of paper.

"Why am I paying you all of this money if you feel like you will lose the case?" I asked waiting for a response.

"All cases are up in the air until all of the evidence is presented. Your friend really hurt our case but we still have a fighting chance. The only other thing that might be weighing on the jurors mind is the conversation your brother had with Agent Jackson about giving you some dope at your business. I still believe I can win this case for you."

"How man? They have Tone, Detective Shaw, pictures of Christian meeting me after he was recorded saying he was bringing me the shit, and the fucking media!"

"Don't lose faith son. After we bring in some people that will defend your character and will testify how

28

good of a citizen you truly are, we will win back the jury. They are on the fence also, believe that. Mr. White are you with me?"

"Man, I am listening to you but I can't lose my woman. You don't know how much shit I have taken her through. Shit she will probably lose it if I was sentenced to 10 or more years," I said sadly. I felt my eyes fill up with tears just imaging her raising my son alone.

"I understand," he replied.

"Man, no you don't understand! She'd just lost her father a few years ago and now she's about to lose me."

"Maurice let me win this case for you!"

"I can't lose man! I can't fucking lose!" I said watching the tears fall down my face.

My lawyer sat and watched me sob, "Well let's do a deal. I can get you a better deal than what they are offering and the judge will agree."

"What's the deal?" I said trying to look him in the eye but the tears burred my vision.

"I will tell them that we will agree to seven years and request that you are housed close to home," the lawyer said writing everything down.

"Damn seven?"

"Seven will be a good offer. Remember you won't have to do the whole seven just 85% of it," he announced looking up from his pad of paper.

"That's still like 6 years man," I said doing the math in my head.

"That's what I can do or we can go down swinging."

"Let's make a deal," I said softly, not truly sure of my answer.

Chapter 3

23 months later

FCI ASHLAND KENTUCKY

     "Lord thank you for allowing me to wake up again. Please protect me and guide me to be a better man today than I was yesterday," I prayed after making my bunk.

     I sat my Bible down next to Diana's and Rico's pictures on my desk and stepped out onto the range. Today I didn't have to work so I decided to go down to the library and read some hometown newspapers. I had to continue my bid how I started. It was the only thing keeping me from losing it in here behind these concrete walls.

     My roommate Deion had to get down to the laundry room because we were getting some stock. The guards woke him up at 5:30 in the morning to unload the truck and store all of the supplies in the laundry unit. Here the guards didn't lift a finger. The inmates made this prison move like a little city behind the walls. We all had a job to do.

     The cold winter air smacked my face like I was just caught grabbing on a random chicks booty. I fixed my snow-hat to cover my ears and stuffed my hands inside of my wool coat. I searched the yard to find any associates but I didn't find any. I didn't like walking the yard period especially alone. I was recognized here as a leader of most of the blacks so I had a few friends but a lot of enemies. Behind these walls I rolled with maybe five or six guys at a time and we were about eighteen deep. I decided against waiting for one of my boys and proceeded to the yard to the library.

When I entered the library, I took off my hat and stumped my boots to get off the few snowflakes that I had on the bottom. The warm air was inviting although the room smelled like bad breath. I'd darted for the newspaper and magazine section. The prison kept the national newspapers and a few local papers for us inmates. Sometimes the papers be days old but we didn't care. News from our streets was well appreciated. I find a seat away from the other inmates and pick up the Cincinnati newspaper.

Today's paper read, "Cincinnati Drug Lord Convicted," in bold letters. The paper had J on the front page. J was in the courtroom getting his sentencing by the federal judge. On the side column of the paper were past pictures of the drugs seized by the cops at his house with another story. I wanted to read the headliner.

I didn't realize at the time but I was a small fish in a big pond. After the prosecutor bagged me and my crew they went after a lot of the dealers connects. I never would have thought that the feds would go after my connect. J was arrested five months after my sentencing. J pleaded guilty and was sentenced to 16 years and 8 months for drug trafficking and another 5 years for importing drugs. Damn he got hit hard, that's almost 22 years of his life and he was around 40 years old. His case had twelve others on the indictment. The U.S. Department of Justice had 52-counts against his crew. The Cincinnati Police, Hamilton County sheriff office and DEA worked together along with Tone snitching ass to get them. J's home was searched, officers recovered 25 kilograms of cocaine, $267,819 in cash, and several phones with other dealer's numbers. The paper read that it was a sealed case until I was indicted. Law enforcements wanted to take down everyone in southwest Ohio that was involved with my case but didn't want J and his crew to become suspicious. I guess they did a good fucking job. Little did they know, there was someone waiting in line soon as we went in.

I left out of the library and headed for my cellblock. Not even before I could get my shadow off of the door I heard someone yelling my name.

"Yo! Yo Reese, you see that shit in the paper homie?" My roommate Deion from Charlotte said running up on me. His dialect was like southern but had the east coast spin on it.

"Yeah man," I answered trying to avoid the conversation.

"The homies told me about it this morning at the chow hall. You are the man around here."

"I don't know if that is a good thing family," I said continuing to walk back to my cell block.

"Shit, it is a wonderful thing," Deion responded blowing on his hands to keep them warm.

"That shit brings attention. These police ass muthafuckas in here will be quick to run their mouths to the guards about it."

"Fuck em!"

"You don't have to worry about shit, you are about to go home in one month," I said aggressively trying to get him to understand where I was coming from.

"Man, I am still in here and until then I am going to ride with you. You was really getting paid back in Ohio huh?"

"I put food on the table."

"That's, that boss shit Reese."

"If that's what you want to call it. I'd just put myself in a position where I could make some money and make sure my house was taken care of."

"I would do it all over again if I was you," Deion said grinning from ear to ear.

"Man six years of my life ain't worth it," I replied with a dead stare.

"Shit you came out good. I got caught with two bricks and a pistol and they gave me 10. Put it like this, if I was getting money like you were, I would do the shit all over again."

"Now I ain't going to bullshit you like I am a rehabilitated man or some shit because push comes to shove I will do it again. But it would be a life or death situation."

"I can dig it," Deion shrugged his shoulders.

"Did you find out about that phone I need yet?"

"No! When C.O. Thurman comes in tonight I am suppose to grab it from him. I don't believe we paid him $500 for a damn phone," Deion said speeding up his pace.

"Make sure that y'all get it and hide it somewhere in the laundry room," I instructed.

"Reese, I got you."

"Don't put my name in this shit either. I don't want anything coming back on me."

"Man we are good. Thurman has brought in more shit than a cheap ass minute phone. I need to introduce y'all to each other. He will be able to get you more shit in here to make your time a lot easier."

"Naw, we are cool. The gambling debts are paying us fairly well," I said grabbing his shoulder to make him stop in his tracks.

"Reese the white boys will continue to run this muthafucka unless you get some dope in here. This place is just like the streets. You will see when the money runs out," Deion philosophized and I knew he was right.

Deion and six more of my boys walked down to the chow hall for the last meal of the evening. A lot of us were excited because today we were having beef-stew, cornbread, green-beans and mashed-potatoes. We rarely received a big meal so everyone was going to the chow hall. I was extra happy because I had a few people that owed me some money but I decided not to take their commissary and have my team eat good instead.

We are in the chow line excited to get this food and some Latin man bumps into me spilling his beef-stew all over my grey pants and new white shoes. I pushed the man hard as hell causing him to slip on the floor landing on his food.

"Watch where you are going muthafucka!" I barked, waiting for him to try to do something.

"Stay your ass down on the floor!" Deion demands standing directly behind him.

The rest of the chow hall erupted with laughter and waited for more action to commence.

"What's going on over there?" A guard asked walking towards us.

Tell him what happened muthafucka!" Deion ordered.

"I will be pass by your cell to get my homies money for some new sneakers later."

We took a seat and begun to eat when I noticed the Latin man sitting all alone. He was shaking and just looked like he was having a nervous breakdown. I hope he didn't think that I was going to touch him over a pair of $40 kicks. I wanted to go over and let him know that it was an accident but my boys would have thought I was growing soft. In here you have to be ready because anybody would test you if they saw any signs of weakness. So I decided to sit still and enjoy my meal.

Suddenly two Hispanic men sit next to him really tightly. He was sitting elbow to elbow with them. The man looked like a human sandwich. He could barely put the spork in his mouth because his hand kept shaking. I studied the man's facial expressions as the other two clearly wanted something from him. He tried to stand up and one of the men grab his shirt pulling him back down to his seat. The men begun to get louder and other convicts near-bye started to tune in on the conversation. I didn't speak much Spanish but I understood 'Peso.' The men kept aggressively asking for pesos. Again the man tried to stand up but this time he is meet with a fist to his abdomen folding him over. They exchange blows to his body violently causing to fall face first to the ground.

"Yeah whoop that muthafuckas ass!" Deion shouts standing in his chair with a mouth full of food.

The two men kicked and stumped on the man until I saw his eyes roll in the back of his head then finally closed. I thought they killed the man. Blood poured out from his mouth and ear. Then suddenly the bigger of the two Hispanic men stumped on his head causing his head to bounce against the floor like a basketball. Blood shot out of his head and continued to leak on the floor.

Whistles blew from the guards charging in the chow hall. They were coming fully loaded and dressed with their combat tactical gear. Their boots hit the pavement sounding like a stampede of bulls charging. The five or six guards that secured the chow all were nowhere in sight.

"Get down!" The guards shouted at the top of their lungs waiving their guns around.

We all hit the floor and spread our hands out. That showed who was aggressive and basically not wanting to get shot. The two Hispanic men didn't stop kicking the shit out of the unconscious man that I had bumped into until the guards where only a few feet away.

"We need a medic!" A member of the tactical team shouted over his radio.

The Hispanic men got snatched up off of their bellies and extracted to the disciplinary block. They were hogged tied and carried out. Before they'd exited the chow hall I'd noticed the big one gave a sign to a group of Hispanics laying on the floor. Right then I knew that it was a hit on that man's life.

Chapter 4

Today started off as a good day. I woke up in a good mood because last night Diana had told me over the phone that she would be coming and she was going to bring Rico today. I hadn't seen my little man since I was in the county awaiting trial.

I kept the cell phone and charger in a Ziploc bag in a huge jug of washing detergent in plain view. The police would never suspect a thing. The only other person that knew of the phone was Deion. He'd rarely used it because most of his people turned their back on him when he'd went down. Even his mother didn't think he was going to do his time and come home. She didn't allow him to parole to her house so he just laid it down and waited to serve out his time. His girlfriend was down at first but after three years of him being incarcerated she dipped. Having the cell phone hidden in the laundry room where I work helped with things back at home.

After eating a load of scrambled eggs, turkey patties, and all of the milk that I could drink, I'd went back to the block. Deion was going home and he could care less for the bullshit we ate so he gave me all of his food and food people owed him. Deion rushed out of the cell and said he would be right back. Deion brought me a new pair of shoes and a laundry bag full of commissary. I gave him a $50 dollar bill I had hidden for the exchange. I knew that he didn't pay for the items from anyone and either hustled someone or flat out took them for me. He didn't take my money that I had offered and he told me that he was just looking out after the many times I had looked out for him.

"Inmate Gadison, pack it up!" A guard shouted coming down the corridor.

"Alright then Reese man. I'll see you when you touchdown. I have your aunt's number so I will stay in touch," Deion said walking out with his few belongings and bedding.

"Stay out of the way family!"

"Peace G. Reese remember to get it how you live. Nobody is going to give you shit in here."

My door was closed back shut for count.

The room felt empty after Deion left. Deion was my roommate for 21 months of my 23 months in the feds. The other two months I was being bounced around being transported till I found this place to be my home. I was wondering how long I could keep the room peaceful so I could get some time to myself. I thought about writing a book on my life and having an empty cell was just what the doctor ordered.

I'd rapidly taped the pen against my desk thinking of what I was going to call the book. I knew that the book was going to tell the truth about the game and my whole life but I didn't know where to start. Every time I would talk to the youngsters on the yard about my old life they would all suggest that I either rapped or wrote a book. Rapping was way out of the question.

Soon as I begun to jot down some ideas I looked up and saw a figure in front of my door. I know that a guard wasn't going to escort me to the visitation room for my visit. I heard the guard radio the control tower to open my door.

Buzz!

"Thurman what's going on?" I asked curiously. I stood up and started for the door to look out onto the range.

"You have some new company," C.O. Thurman said stepping back to allow a new inmate in.

I couldn't see the man's face because he had his mattress blocking my view. I didn't want a new roommate. I tried to step around the man and talk to Thurman but the door closed soon as I had opened my mouth.

"Thurman! Come on man. Damn can I get just one muthafucking day to my damn self. Fuck!" I shouted through the door but Thurman ignored me continuing to walk down the range.

"I want be here for long chamo. You don't have to worry about me," the man spoke with a deep Spanish dialect.

I turned around and to my surprise it's the Latin man that bumped into me at the chow hall. I guess he was finally released from the medical unit. I heard he was beaten up badly but those rumors were over exaggerated. I could only see a scare across his nose and what was left of a black eye. The purple mark in the corner of his eye was fading away.

"My name is Juan Michael Estrada senor," the man said sticking out his hand for me to greet him.

I shook his hand firmly putting away our race differences.

"I am Reese."

"I want be a in your way senor. I only have 5 more months left then I would be released."

"Wow, you speak English pretty well sir. I can tell that you are not from here," I said taking a seat on the chair.

"No senor! I am from Venezuela."

"Damn I never met anyone from there before. You are a long ways from home," I replied shocked to hear that he wasn't from Mexico.

"I actually live in Puerto Rico now."

"I heard that there are some beautiful women out there. I am going to definitely visit that place one day. Hopefully as soon as I get out."

"Yes it is a beautiful place," he'd answered nodding his head yes. Look as if he was fantasizing about the country.

"Might I ask you a question?"

"Go ahead."

"Why did those men beat you? Did you happen to bump into them also?"

We both laughed.

"No senor. Those men are friends of a cartel in Mexico and they know I am in here all alone."

"They must want something from you."

"They want me to pay for protection."

"Protection from who?"

"You!"

"Me?" I questioned confused by his words.

He must have noticed my facial expressions because he quickly stopped fixing his bed and looked directly at me. He took a deep breath before he'd continued.

"No disrespect but Blacks. Whites. Even most Mexicans."

"Why do you need to be protected?" I wondered.

"It's no secret but I run the imports and exports of a lot of the drugs coming from my country to Puerto Rico. I make sure that the boats complete their drops and the product is shipped to America."

I hopped up from my seat and allowed the man to take the seat. I wanted to know more about this man because he was speaking my language.

Bird talk.

"What kind of dope?" I asked curiously wanting to know more about the international dope game. This shit was real money. Ideas begun to run through my head like I was a mad scientists.

"My familia in Venezuela makes the cocaina, package it and put it on the boats for fishermen. They act like they are fishing in the day wading in the Caribbean waters and speed to the coast of Puerto Rico at night."

"How in the hell are y'all not getting caught by the coast guard or DEA?" I asked anticipating to hear his answer.

"The speedboats looks just like another fishing boat or sometimes if it's a large shipment we will cover the boat with a dark tarp to hide from helicopters. At night they are speeding across the water to get me the drugs."

"Damn! You just said some shit. I had a connect from Hatti but I was still paying a large price for the shit."

"Most of the Hatti dealers get their drugs from the Columbians or us but we normally sell the drugs to the amigos in The Dominican Republic. Then they will get it to them. You are paying for all of the risks of the transport."

"Most of the times I just mail the drugs to someone in the states because once the drugs are in Puerto Rico I don't have to worry about customs."

"Wow! I will be eating because I know a lot of people that would love to get some good quality dope for the low. I have folks all over Ohio, Kentucky, North

Carolina, and up in Detroit that will be eager to get their hands on some good shit."

"You are right chamo."

C.O. Thurman poked his head in the widow. Once again greeted me at the door. This time he was here to tell me that my visitor was here. I rapidly marched to the visitation room cheerfully to see my family.

Chapter 5

After being searched to go into the visitation room, I am allowed in. Diana and Rico sat in the plastic chairs waiting to see me. Rico didn't hesitate to run into my arms. I am brought to tears seeing the level of joy my son has for me. I gave him a huge hug and kiss on his cheek.

"Love you daddy!" Rico shouted excitedly. He hugged my neck tighter.

I looked around Rico's head and Diana was standing waiting for her love. I stretched my arms open allowing her to get in our group hug. Diana stood on the tip of her toes and lifted her chin for me kiss her. Diana planted a long juicy kiss on my lips. The taste of her lip gloss tasted like warm apple pie. I wanted more but the female guard kept her eyes on us and I didn't want to lose my visitation privileges.

I licked my lips imagining kissing her in our bedroom. I am laid up against the soft pillows and watched her crawl across our king sized bed. Diana straddled me wearing nothing but a pair of earrings and a diamond necklace. She massages my chest with her lips until her lips reach mine. I grabbed her ass tightly digging my fingers into her soft caramel skin.

"Reese, let's sit down and talk," Diana said waking me up from my trance like state.

"You look good baby," I said smiling like a kid standing in line to see Santa Claus.

"You do to. Seems like you have gained a little more muscles since the last time I had came down to see you."

"Your man have been doing his thing on the weights really seriously lately," I continued to smile.

"Is that a new tattoo?" Diana asked looking at my forearm.

I turned my arm so that she could see the tattoo clearly. "Yes. I wanted something I could remember my brother by."

"That's nice," she said almost crying. Her voice quivered as she spoke.

"Rico let me and your mom talk for a little bit. Why don't you go over there and find a book for me to read you."

"Yay!" Rico said running off.

"So what's up? How are you holding up?" I asked trying to really get the truth from her. Anyone could tell you anything over the phone but their body language would tell the truth.

"We are okay. Rico is talking about you every day wondering when you are going to come home. His teachers love him."

"That's good to hear. But I really want to know how you are holding up? Did you pick up some money from my auntie to get you down here?

"No she didn't have it either. Guess who I got the money from?"

"Who?" I asked curiously. I talked to Sky last week and she said she would drop some money in the mailbox for Diana without her finding out. Sky had really been doing her part to hold me down. Sky took some of her earning to Diana's mother's house every Sunday morning when I knew Diana would be at church. Sky would simply put the money in an envelope and drop it in the mailbox.

"B! He made parole three days ago. I wanted to give you some good news face to face."

"Damn! That was fast."

"He came right over asking about you. I told him that you only had a little while left to go and he was excited. He'd offered to help any way he could. So I asked him for some money and he gave me $400. He also took Rico shopping and bought him all types of stuff."

"Okay."

"He's living with a stripper named Sky."

The bitch didn't mention B staying with her.

"Why ain't he with his girl?" I questioned waiting for her response.

"Ashley knew that he wasn't going to come home and act right so she moved on. She's now engaged to a construction worker in Columbus."

"Damn that's fucked up!"

"How is it? You know B."

"Right."

"He's not looking like he is sad about it. I guess the young girl is giving him what he needs."

"Maybe so," I said softly.

"Reese are you ok? I would have thought that knowing B was released would have lifted your spirits," Diana asked. She grabbed my face to look at me.

"Inmate!" the female officer shouted.

"I'm sorry," Diana replied waving at the lady.

"She's tripping. No guard in here be on it like that," I said agitated.

"I also wanted to tell you about momma," Diana said shaking her legs.

I took her hands and held them waiting for her to speak.

"My momma isn't doing really well baby. Soon as my father died I seen it in her. She is slowly dying without him. The doctors said that she has heart disease and only time will tell. Her heart can't heal because my father isn't here. It kills me seeing her like that," Diana wept.

"I know it does," I snuck to wipe her eyes and give her another kiss.

"Everything is just weighing all on me. I am tired of it Reese. I don't know how much I can take," Diana cried.

I allowed her to put her head on my shoulder and continue to cry. "I will find a way to make things better for you, I promise."

"How are you going to do that from in here?" She asked trying to stop from crying. Diana looked up at me trying to read my face for my answer.

"I will make something happen."

Diana let go of my hand, "Reese things ain't as easy as you think. I am taking care of my mom, Rico and trying to stay strong for you. But I can't take much more. I can barely pay for Rico's clothes. It seems as if he is growing every day. I am raising him all alone."

I found Rico in the children's room playing with some cars. He was in his own little world. Not a care in the world. What I would do just to be with him again. Time away from him was killing me.

"I will have one of my youngsters shoot you some money to help out asap," I said trying to grab her hand but she'd snapped back.

"Reese your friends haven't given me anything in a while. The only person to help us was B. They don't stop by or even look my way when I see them out. No one is going to help us but us!"

"Let me figure out some things," I said quietly avoiding eye contact. Honestly I didn't know what to do.

"Well while you're trying to figure things out I have to make sure Rico has food in his stomach and shoes on his feet," Diana snapped with an attitude. She rolled her eyes and smacked her lips like I was just some lame.

"Listen! I can only do what I can do from in here. I told you that I would find a way. What else do you want me to do?"

"I didn't know that I was going to be married to you and the game. Your mistakes has affected us! We are close to losing everything!"

"Like what?" I questioned becoming furious.

"Are you serious Reese? I had to sell the laundromat and both of our cars. I am now riding in my mother's twenty year car. I used to have a fifty thousand dollar car and now I don't have shit!"

"You still have the house," I replied.

"Yeah a house that I don't even live in," Diana again smacked her lips. She grabbed her purse and threw the stapes over her shoulder like she was ready to go.

"At least we still have it and those people are helping you out on a few dollars from paying rent."

"Reese I am just saying that I don't know if I can handle much more of this. If it wasn't for B we wouldn't even be here today."

"I am going to be able to help you really soon..." I said but was quickly cut off before I could continue what I was saying.

"I can't deal with this shit Reese. I quit my hundred thousand dollar a year job because you told me that you wanted me to stay home and raise Rico but you never thought about what would happen to us if you went to prison."

"I can't take this shit right now Diana," I said sadly.

"With everything going on with my mom and trying to provide for Rico, I just don't think we should come visit until we get back on our feet."

I took my hands and covered my face to hide the pain I was feeling. "Diana you don't have to bullshit me. If you want a divorce I will understand. You want have any trouble and I will give you the house. It pains me to be away from you and him and it hurts deeply to hear you struggle."

"Why would you say that? You are my king. I know that this day will past. It's just the struggle is crazy," Diana said pulling away my hands.

"Thank you. Know that I will always love you. I promise that this struggle will be over soon."

"Reese..." Diana said but I cut her off.

"You are right. I don't want you to come down until we can afford it. I understand. Trust me I do. We will get everything back that we had lost."

"Visitation is now over!" The female correctional officer said.

"Damn that was fast!" I barked standing up.

"Rico come say goodbye to your daddy," Diana said getting up from her seat.

Rico ran across the tan tile floor like an Olympic sprinter. I picked him up and hugged him and kissed him all over. Rico laughed and tried to avoid the kisses.

"Visitation is over inmate!" The female officer shouted walking towards us with another guard.

"This is my son give me a minute!" I shouted back positioning myself to stand directly facing them.

"Reese it's okay baby. You don't need to get in any trouble," Diana spoke up looking the guards over. "Rico let's go. You will talk to your daddy later."

I walked away peacefully but it took everything in me not to buck on the police. I didn't want to make my time more miserable by spending it in the hole. More importantly I didn't want my son seeing his father abused by the police so I just walked away.

"Inmate White! The next time I see you breaking the visitation rules, I will have your ass in the hole so fast you won't know what happened. Now go dress out." She ordered.

I starred her down and then my eyes scrolled down to her breast. I read her name tag. Officer J. Lopez. I giggled at her name with the thought of the actor slash musician. The officer did resemble her but her attitude was funky. I wanted to smack the shit out of her but I decided against it knowing the repercussions.

I left the visitation room with mixed emotions. Seeing my baby hurt was killing me. I had to get her life together fast and that was by any means necessary.

CHAPTER 6

"How was your visit?" Juan asked looking up from his Bible when I entered the cell.

"It was okay."

"You seem down chamo," Juan said sitting his Bible down on his bunk.

He climbed down off his bed and his bare feet smacked against the cold floor. He took a seat waiting for me to discuss more.

"Juan my life is crumbling down. My wife is miserable without me. We have lost everything and I feel like I am losing her," I confessed shaking my head with disbelief.

"Sorry to hear about that."

"Man, my wife is struggling to take care of her mom, herself and my son. I can't get her enough money to keep her afloat. The little money that I do get her is only enough to pay for a few bills and daycare."

"I can help you chamo," Juan uttered.

"Juan I'll find a way man. Thanks but no thanks. I'll always find a way," I replied laying down in the bed to get my mind together.

"I have a way my friend."

"You know what fuck it. I am listening," I said popping up from my relaxed position.

"I don't have access to money in here but I can get you more product than you could ever imagine at a price only you can imagine. I can make it to where you can just sit back and count cash."

Juan and I continued to talk about our lives and how we had ended up here. Juan and I had more in common than I thought. We both were married and had kids. Juan was also the same age as I. In fact, the more we'd talked the more we cliqued. Juan told me that his wife and children were also living poorly back at home. Sadly he said that his wife had turned to the one thing that got him in here. Drugs.

Juan told me that he had gotten caught up at a stash house at the wrong time. The Miami Dade Police had gotten word of the stash house and was watching it for a while. Juan called the men at the stash letting them know that he was going to personally pick up the cash for the drugs he sold a week earlier. Less than five minutes after going inside, he walked out of the stash house and guns were all in his face.

Juan was busted with over $800,000 cash. Miami Dade Police didn't blow up his case because their police force was used to this amount and much more they have seized. Juan protected himself with a good lawyer and received the minimum on his charges. I felt exactly like Deion when he said he would do it all over again if he was in my shoes. Shit I know Juan was getting that money.

Getting caught with that amount only tells me how much dope he had.

Juan and I continued to talk for about four more hours. I honestly believed everything he was saying. Shit what he needed to lie for. I knew that the Mexican's wanted him for something and more than likely it was dope. They'd probably wanted for him to get some dope either in here or on the streets. Protection my ass. They wanted to protect a sure thing. With the cartel losing millions of dollars trying to send mules and truck drivers across the boarder, they were rapidly thinking of other ways to get their drugs into the United States. Getting their dope to Puerto Rico was the next best thing.

Juan really got my attention when he started talking about his family. Juan had five kids and his oldest son at the young age of thirteen already had a position in the drug import export business. Juan had been selling dope since he was nine years old when his father was a manufacturer in Venezuela. They called themselves farmers. I would love to farm over there. He said it was a family business but they were not getting money like I would imagine. His move to the island paid beneficial to him and his family. His first two years on the island Juan worked as a fisherman collecting all of the information he needed. At the age of sixteen he met his Puerto Rican wife.

He was literally married to the game. Juan's wife was the daughter of the drug kingpin that bought the dope from the Venezuelan fishermen and shipped it to the states. They were a perfect match for their family's success. Juan took over his father-in-law business shortly after the man passed away. His wife's brother took most of the men with him and they were Juan's protection. His bother in law was the muscle for the family and Juan was the brains. Juan had people from the police, customs, fishermen, the U.S. Coast Guard, and local businesses to hide the dope before either being mailed or shipped wherever.

Before we knew it, it was time for evening chow. We stepped out together on the range. Juan looked nervous as hell. I searched frantically with my eyes for a few of my boys. I found Slick and RJ. I'd signaled for them to wait for me outside of the door.

"What's good Reese?" RJ asked in his baritone voice.

"You know the homie Deion left today?" I responded, but I knowingly knew what he was talking about.

Juan stood right next to me like a statue not saying a word or moving at all.

"This is my new roommate. We are going to make sure that my roommate don't have any more problems with the Mexicans."

"You want us to protect him from his own people?" Slick said screwing up his face. He looked Juan up and down in disgust. He'd stepped to Juan like he was ready to knock his ass out.

"Yes I do!" I raised my voice stepping in-between him and Juan.

"Why?" Slick asked stepping back to stand near RJ.

"Because I asked you to. I have mutual interest in him as well as the Mexicans."

"Man I do not know. This can lead to a war in here why we are protecting a muthafucka that ain't even our people," RJ spoke brushing his waves in his head.

I looked over Slick's shoulder and noticed two of my homies from home walking towards us. I wanted them to get in on this conversation also but I wanted them to back me so that everyone else would. One thing about Ohio folks in prison is that we come together despite our differences.

Demarco was from Cincinnati and Ed was from Toledo. Demarco and I was the closes not because of the distance of our neighboring cities but he also was buying work from J. Demarco respected me and I respected him.

I must have ran into Demarco four or five times when I went over to J's to pick up some dope. We both walked out with dumb size bags full of dope. Demarco was a Blood and ran with a crew on Harrison Ave. His crew also made plays in downtown Cincinnati. Demarco left the streets filled with dope and his crew made sure he was living good for his six year bid. Demarco didn't bother with trying to get money inside but he wasn't afraid of betting on games or playing basketball for cash although he didn't need it. It was just hard to get the hustle out of any of us that knew the fast life of the dope game. Even when I was laid up in the bed not able to walk from my gun wounds, Demarco would tell Christian that he said what up and get well.

"Listen, I want everyone to put the word out that we are protecting this man," I said pointing at Juan.

"Him?" They both said in unison.

RJ laughed.

"That's what I said," Slick interjected as he'd greeted the two of them with a handshake.

"Man listen. I don't want nobody fucking with him period. I owe this man a favor and I am going to repay him by providing him some protection. Once they see him with us they will know what time it is."

"Shit he owes you some shoes," RJ continued to laugh.

"That's behind me. Shit that's petty as fuck. The man apologized and that was the end of it," I said defending myself.

"Reese you are my dude so you know that I got you. I will pass the word that we are protecting him," Demarco stated firmly.

"Nobody will fuck with him I will make sure of it," Ed added giving me a handshake.

"Slick if everything work like I believe it will, you will be able to come home to some money or have it in here," I said throwing my arm around Slick's shoulder and proceeding to walk to the chow hall.

"If you can really get me together I want you to prove it. I want you to call your folks and have them get it to my people on the streets."

"Chamo, I can't use these telephones in here," Juan confessed.

"Don't worry about that, I will handle that little problem for you man," I said patting Juan on the back.

At that moment I had an idea for Juan to mail something to Sky and have B get rid of it for me while I was in here. This way I would be able to take care of my responsibilities at home and keep money rolling in here. Deion was right about me taking what was mine. Nobody wasn't going to give me shit in here nor from home. I had to get it how I live. Straight hustling.

By the time we were about to enter the chow hall it's like a dozen of us. Demarco signaled for the fellas to gather up and we entered the chow hall like a small army. Slick kept a sharp tool on him from the time he was jumped in the state joint about five years ago. Slick was a skinny ass dude but he had hands for his size. He just got out of the hole for fighting. A few of the others had weapons on them also just in case some shit jumped off.

The chow hall was running like normal. The whites sat with the whites, the blacks with the blacks, and everybody else in their own little section. Juan and I entered together and I made sure that he felt protected.

As we were served our food the chow fell silent. I noticed the whites looking over at us and then waited for the Mexican's response. The Mexicans started talking amongst themselves in Spanish but they knew we had them out numbered.

I watched the room closely while everyone quietly ate and watched us. Juan ate like a king. He smiled and didn't have a care in the world. He was confident and was talking amongst the fellas like he was one of the boys. Juan had a breath of fresh air. His protection had arrived and his fear was over. While everyone was being friendly and enjoying their meal Ed and I was on guard duty. At any moment somebody could've walked up on us and tried to stab up any of the members of the clique. I wasn't going to allow that to happen. I barely touched my food as I continued to observe the hall.

After chow I pulled Thurman to the side and asked him to move Juan to the laundry room with me. I wanted Juan to stay right by my side until he was released. Thurman told me he would see what he could do but I knew he was going to make it happen. I gave him my only cash, the fifty dollar bill and walked away without a doubt in my mind that Juan will have a job change by the morning.

Later on that evening, I was able to make the call to Diana and tell her that I had a plan in motion. She wasn't surprised to hear that I was back in the game doing what I was built to do. She had reminded me all that I had lost behind this game but all I could think about was what I had left to lose.

I also called Sky. She didn't answer the first time I called so I called again. She finally picked up on the second call. I heard B in the background but I didn't trip. I guess she went somewhere quiet so I wouldn't assume she was fucking some nigga but little did she know that I was already on game. Sky stuttered as soon as she'd picked up the phone. She thought I was mad at her about not putting some money in the mailbox for Diana. I canceled that noise and started the conversation how I wanted it to go. I told her that I knew that B was living there and she busted in tears. She claimed that B forced himself to move in because he didn't have anywhere else to go. I wasn't trying to hear that shit. She was just a bitch that I fucked and that was it. I had a queen waiting for me at home. There wasn't any love lost. I told her that I would be mailing her a gift from a friend and to show my appreciation. She became excited until I told her that B should put it together for her. She instantly got an attitude because she knew that I was done with her. I still controlled her mentally and asked her to continue to look out for Diana and she'd assured me she would. Before we had ended our call I ordered her to put B on the phone. She reluctantly did what she was told.

"Who is this?" B shouted into the phone sounding drunk as hell.

"It's your brother," I answered trying to make sure no one was listening to my conversation.

"Reese! What up boy? How you get this number?" B said excitedly.

"I had it for a while," I answered quickly.

"Are y'all two still talking after that night? Fam I didn't know. The bitch didn't say shit," B rambled not allowing me to get a word in.

"B you are my boy. You should know that I am not tripping. Shit she is a free woman and is able to make her own decision."

"You are right about that. Anyways you are a married man."

"Exactly!"

"Yeah, Diana said she was going to see you today. I had Sky give me some money to give to Diana."

"I appreciate that man," I replied.

"Don't worry about it. Shit Sky is over there making some shit at the strip club," B said nonchalantly not caring about Sky at all.

"Well thanks for looking out. She did come and she brought my lil man with her. It felt great holding them in my arms. You notice how big Rico has gotten?"

"Yeah I noticed. He wears like a size 2 in gym shoes already. Time is flying by. I remember when she was pregnant with him," B replied.

"You remember that?"

"Of course I do," B answered.

"Diana got big as fuck over those few months. All she did was eat and eat some more."

"Well she' not like that anymore. Diana has gotten back in shape man. You couldn't tell?" B asked.

"Hell yeah I noticed fool. I was all over her ass in the visitation room until the guard started talking shit."

"Damn for real?" B laughed.

"Hell yeah. Well check this out. You are the only one I have left that I can trust. I am going to send you a gift of my appreciation to you soon. All I ask you in return is to look out for Diana."

"Enough said. Good looking Reese. I need to get back on my feet."

"Alright then man. I will call you again tomorrow or so just be on the lookout," I said ending the call.

When I entered back into the cell Juan was laying back on his bed reading a western novel. I didn't see what he'd liked about those books but that was his thing. I informed him that he would be working with me in the morning and he needed to make that call. He'd agreed and laid back down like it wasn't nothing.

The game plan was on.

Chapter 7

Juan and I were working side by side folding laundry when he whispered in my ear asking to use the phone to make the call to his people. I watched everyone closely making sure that they didn't see me taking out the phone. I secured the phone and skillfully placed it in Juan's right pocket. I signaled with my eyes that he had the phone and it was clear for him to make the call. I give him a note with Sky's address. He walked behind the large industrial size washers and quickly made the call.

While Juan was on the phone I made sure that nobody went near him or tried to be nosey. I stood close by Juan pretending to be some sort of guard. Luckily no one didn't disturb him or ask any questions.

Juan walked back out and nodded his head assuring me that the job was done. He tried to do my move by trying to place the phone in my pocket but it slipped down my leg and onto the floor. The noise alone caused me to become nervous. I looked around to see if anyone saw the phone slide across the floor into a pile of dirty laundry. I took a deep breath and thanked God that the noise didn't catch anyone's attention.

I rushed over to the phone and stuffed it in my pants. I turned to place the phone back into the secret hidden spot and Demarco stood right behind me.

"What's good Reese?" He asked with his hands out.

"Shit nothing. I'm ready to get out of this bitch."

"I am to."

"Are you hitting the yard latter?"

"You know I am. I have to get my body right for all of the honeys back at home. You feel me?" Demarco said shaking my hand and smiling showing his gold grill.

"Well, I will meet you out there," I said walking away towards my hiding spot.

"Reese, you need this?" Demarco said holding the Ziploc bag.

Damn! Now he knows about the phone. Demarco was cool but I wanted to keep this on the low. I didn't want everybody on my phone like some phone sex hotline. I'd only hoped that he would keep this phone shit on the low low. If not him and I would be coming to blows. The phone kept me close with my family and after Diana decided not to come here for a while this would be all I have besides pen and paper.

After work we all meet up outside on the yard and decide to get a little work out in. It was cool to hit the weights but we liked doing calisthenics. The weather was great and the fellas were all ready to get their workout on. Juan even decided to get it in with us. He normally would do some pushups and sit-ups with me in the cell but today he really wanted to get it in.

We all partnered up and started to work out but from the corner of my eye I see Demarco coming out of his shirt. I thought that maybe he was doing this to become a little bit more loose. Something told me to turn all of the way around. I looked and Demarco was stepping to one of the Mexican men that jumped Juan a while ago.

"Get the fuck away from here homeboy!" Demarco shouted flexing his chest muscles.

"No way. I'm not fucking going anywhere!" He said.

Slick, Ed, RJ and the rest of the fellas took noticed and stopped what they were doing to back Demarco.

"Go over there with your folks," RJ said getting everyone attention with his deep voice.

RJ didn't speak much but when he did people listened.

The man stood firm. He looked over his shoulder for his friends and only two of them had the balls to come and back him. They didn't get near their friend before RJ hit him with a right hook to the face. The man stumbled left and fell out backwards. I hopped up but Demarco signaled for me to fall back. The other two men stopped dead in their tracks. A heavy set guard who was patrolling nearby frantically hauled ass towards us.

"Everybody back the fuck up!" The guard shouted. He rapidly searched for help and calmed down when he saw four more guards rushing. "What happened here?" The guard asked looking at both groups.

The Hispanic man woke up out of quick nap. He held his jaw like it was a chinstrap. His eyes were glossy and his bottom lip had a small cut. He took a deep breath and managed to get up to his knees before the guards assisted. He continued to hold his jaw but gave RJ a look that could kill.

"Well what the fuck happened to him!" The guard shouted aggressively. He put his hand on his nightstick and stared us down knowing that we had something to do with it.

"I guess he had passed out from working out boss man," Slick finally spoke up.

We all chuckled.

Slick didn't give a fuck. He stayed in the hole or on some type of restrictions because of his behavior.

"Somebody will tell me something sooner or later," the guard added helping the Hispanic man to his feet. "Are you ok?"

"Yeah man," he answered walking away.

"You need a medic?" Another guard asked.

The Hispanic man continued to walk away ignoring the guards trying to check him out. The other two followed right behind him also not saying a word.

I wished everyone was built like this.

We continued our workout session uninterrupted. The guards stood close talking amongst themselves. Their eyes studied our every movement. I didn't know if they were protecting us or waiting for us to go dumb.

I went over to RJ and told him that I will give him some commissary for looking out for my cellmate. He was happy. RJ wasn't getting much money in here either. He told me that it was just hard for his folks to accept his collect phone calls because money was tight. I was thinking about putting him on to my secret phone but time would tell.

RJ was in here for robbing drug dealers. RJ was from ST. Louis but traveled the whole Midwest robbing. RJ was a young cat only 24 years old. He had been locked up for seven years with three more to go. Unluckily RJ had went on a robbing spree in Kentucky and Southern Indiana and accidently robbed an undercover DEA agent. Young and wild, RJ and two of his home boys held the cop at gunpoint until the cop revealed where the stash of cash was. Even after the agent told them where the money was at RJ beat him up badly to show off his muscle. RJ was on the run for only a week until his then girlfriend turned him in for a measly $10,000 reward. RJ's luck continued to get worst when both of his home boys took the stand against him. His girlfriend wouldn't have known shit if he wasn't telling her every time he'd hit a lick on somebody. He was rumored to have stashed $500,000 thousand somewhere before getting caught but it wasn't worth it in my eyes.

After working out, we all went in our blocks to get ready to take showers. It took me a little longer than anticipated because I was getting a few commissary items together for RJ. I threw the items in a bag and grabbed my shower items and suddenly I heard the guard whistles blowing, sirens, and then they ordered us to lock down.

What the fuck happened?

A few hours past and I was rapidly pacing my cell room floor. I had to find out what was going on because I knew that it was something bad. I knew that it had something to do with what happened on the yard. The idea of something happened to one of my boys ran through my mind rapidly.

Juan didn't give a fuck about what was going on outside of this cell. He laid on his bed reading the Bible like he was studying to be a priest. This shit happened because of him. We didn't have any problems with anyone until I decided to watch over him. I stood looking out of my door for any sight of information or catch the guards talking. Not one guard came by. I checked my watch and noticed that it was time for lights out. I was really pissed. I knew that by the morning we would have to plan on our retaliation or we would all be haunted down like dogs in the street.

Not able to sleep, I stayed up in deep contemplation. Although we'd outnumbered the Mexicans I knew that they would go to war with us giving it everything they got. The war wouldn't just affect us in here but life on the streets. Our families could be potentially at risk.

Suddenly I heard the sounds of boots charging into the cell block. I checked my watch and it was 3:17 in the morning. I quickly pulled my T-shirt over my head and threw on my jogging pants. I peeked outside the cell door and the army of guards were on their way.

Lights turned on awaking the whole block.

"Get up and get out!" Guards shouted with their combat equipment on.

Juan jumped up from his bed like he was on fire. I had let out a giggle watching his behavior. A guard that I didn't recognized thought that I was laughing at them so they decided to get a little rough with me.

Two guards wrestled me down to the ground, "What's so fucking funny inmate!"

I ignored them but they continued to shout in my ear. I looked down the range and I was not alone. A few others were being roughed up by these guards for whatever reason. I guess the guards wanted to strike fear in us but a lot of us wasn't buying what they were selling.

Juan exited the room and they picked me up and forcefully escorted us away from our cells. Guards entered our cell and begun trashing each of them. It looked like a riot in the block. Clothes, food, bedding and trash was thrown out of the room. I did figure out that these guards were looking for something in particular because they were only really harassing the Mexicans and us. The white inmates were just patted down and escorted out the cell block. The rest of us were on their radar. I just prayed that they didn't mess with my pictures of my family. I would be highly pissed and they will know it.

When we were allowed to enter back into the cell block many of the inmates roared with anger. We had noticed that a few of us were missing. Guards had taken a few inmates to the disciplinary dorm for having contraband. The guards had the day room table full with tattoo guns, a few cell phones, bags of tobacco, porno pictures and petty stuff like broken combs.

The guards left out taking all of the contraband. They left us a block full of trash to clean and the attention of every guard in the institution. I was going to be cautious with every move I made from now on.

Juan entered our cell first and his bed was unbelievably in perfect condition but they destroyed my bed. My bedding was on the floor but I wasn't tripping because I was going to bounce back and get a brand new set today. I was just happy to see that my pictures were in place without damages.

Juan and I fixed up the cell to perfection. It was nice having a cell mate that was on keeping the room clean like I was. Sometimes Deion would leave plastic wrappers under his mattress for days until the wrappers accidently found the floor. That's when he would decide to clean.

After cleaning our room it was time for breakfast then work. The institution was on a controlled movement.

We were only allowed to be in specific destinations and the guards walked with us everywhere. The chow hall was so quiet you could hear the pots and pans chiming in the kitchen.

The institution was on a lockdown. No showers. No phones. No commissary. No recreation time. Not a damn thing. Only thing that was moving in this place were the cooks, laundry workers, and guards.

I had to find out what happened to Slick and RJ. People were talking about the fight but the stories were all over the place. I heard that RJ and Slick died. I heard the Mexican that RJ knocked out had razor bladed RJ's face so bad that muscles were falling out of his face. I had to get down to the truth because these jailhouse stories were bullshit.

On our way to the laundry room, I saw Demarco walking ahead of us. He had a look of disbelief written all over his face. I wondered if he'd heard anything about RJ or Slick. I stopped walking and saw C.O. Thurman walking towards us. I had to get some information.

"Officer Thurman, can I have a word with you sir?" I asked sounding like a respected inmate.

"Yes. How may I help you sir."

Thurman and I walked side by side heading for the laundry room. We kept our voices low so that our conversation wouldn't be heard by unwanted ears. Thurman told me everything he knew but expected a payment for this information. I didn't have much to give but a promise. Thurman didn't like that at all and he'd promised to put some heat on me if I didn't fatten his pockets.

I had to think of a way to pay him fast. I needed a dirty muthaucka on my side in here.

Receiving the information from Thurman had me ready to go into the war room and get every black man in here ready for war. Thurman said that after the fight in the shower, that RJ was sent to the local hospital because his injuries were too severe. He believed that RJ died on his way to the hospital but he wasn't for sure. Thurman also said that Slick received a few minor injuries and he was in the med unit being treated. Slick would be out in a day or two but would be held in protective custody until they find out exactly what happened. He couldn't tell me for sure what had happened because as of now Silk was the only witness. We had to wait. He did admit that the guards believed that the fight carried over because of the fight in the yard. He'd also admitted that our cell block along with another were searched because RJ was cut with something very sharp and the guards couldn't risk having that tool in the institution.

Thurman walked me to the laundry room then departed to go on his assigned duty. With two of my enforcers not available it would be hard to get some of the people who owed money to pay without a fight. I either had to take a lost or find a way to get more money in here to take care of everyone.

Soon as I entered the laundry room Demarco rushed me. He didn't know much about the fight either but was eager to know if I had any information. I told him what I was told by Thurman. He was surprised to hear what I had told him because he had seen RJ handle two to three men with his bare hands at times. I haven't known RJ long but I have witnessed him knocking out a few folks and never backed down from a confrontation. Demarco said that a few of the boys were ready to act but I told him that wouldn't be wise. The police were ready and more importantly we didn't have all of the facts. He understood and walked away to go back to work.

"Can I make that call Reese?" Juan asked.

"Wait let me find out who's the guard on duty first then I will get you together?"

I walked around the laundry room looking for the guard on duty. Normally the guard would drop in and out of the laundry room just to do their job. All of us were never any trouble for the guards so they rarely bothered us. The only time they kept eyes on us was when we had a shipment we had to pull off the truck.

Not knowing who the officer was on duty I decided against pulling out the phone. I kept looking over at my stash spot weighing out when should I take the phone out. Juan asked me again but I told him that I had to take care of something first. I took the push-broom from the storage closet and brushed the floor waiting to see the guard.

While I am barely collecting dust, Officer J. Lopez entered the laundry room. Our eyes locked for a moment.

I looked in her hazel eyes and studied her body up and down. She took a seat near Demarco and watched him dry bed linen. I was surprised to see her in here with a bunch of men all alone. I knew that she would watch us like a hawk. I pushed the broom right by her purposely trying to get her attention.

I was so close that I could smell her perfume.

"Inmate White," she said standing to her feet.

Damn she'd remembered my name.

"Yes?"

"You missed a spot," she'd pointed at a piece of lent on the floor.

"I'm not getting that little piece of lent," I chuckled.

"What?" She asked walking towards me.

"What do you mean? That shit ain't hurting anybody. The floor is practically spotless."

"Inmate White come here," she said walking away from everybody.

I followed her near the back door where we get our shipments from. I noticed that she was making sure that we were under the camera.

"Why are you always testing me sir?" She asked after taking a sip from her water bottle.

"I'm not testing you Ms. Lopez."

"Officer Lopez," she spoke up.

Officer Lopez walked away a few steps going back towards the main room. I watched her step away and something gave me the courage to step to her. Maybe it was the way she'd swayed her hips. Maybe it was the way she'd looked at me. Maybe it was her curvy Latin body. Fuck it. I had to have her.

"Officer Lopez, I haven't been truly honest with you," I uttered getting right in front of her.

"I figured that Mr. White," she blushed.

I am sure she was wet with the thought of fucking me.

"Did you?"

"Yes."

"So how I can we make my fantasy a reality?" I asked reaching around and grabbing on her ass.

Her ass wasn't super fat but it was fat enough to take some dick. Her sassy attitude and thick lips attracted me. I loved a boss chic.

"Is this a test or do you really want to taste this pussy?" She asked seductively.

"This is not a test Officer Lopez," I said softly breathing on her neck.

I whispered in her ear to meet me in the storage closet away from the cameras and she can grade me on how good this dick is. I told her that if she wasn't playing any games that she should meet me in the closet within five minutes.

I went in the closet and placed the broom in its proper place. I moved the mop bucket and some laundry supplies out of the way just in case she'd took me up on my offer. I was making all types of noise but I knew that everyone was occupied and couldn't hear me over all of those machines and music playing.

Officer Lopez opened the door and hurriedly closed the door. She wasn't smiling or giving me a look of seduction. Her face was serious like I was on the other end of the badge. She looked at me like she knew she was going to handle her business.

She inched closer to me and grabbed my shaft firmly. Finally I got a smile out of her. She was so close that I could smell the sweet scent of her perfume. Without any hesitation she'd dropped to her knees and pulled my dick out. My man was standing erect at attention knowing what was about to go down. She had to maneuver my waistband on my boxers around my dick because it was so hard. Officer Lopez wrapped her black manicured finger nails around my shaft and stroked it firmly. I leaned up against the wall and closed my eyes enjoying her touch. She begun to play with my balls with her free hand and then took me in her mouth. She stroked and sucked on my dick simultaneously. I combed my fingers through her curly auburn hair. Lopez begun to go hard on the dick sucking me faster and faster. Her tongue swirled and sucked on my shaft like a hurricane. I forcefully grabbed her by the back of her head and stuffed her face down so she can try to get all of me down her throat. Surprisingly she didn't choke or try to come up. She continued to show me her head game. Not having sex in years, I ended up bursting in the back of her throat accidently. Officer Lopez didn't allow a drop to hit the floor. I let go of her curls after I finished allowing her to stand up.

"Your job isn't over Inmate White," she said unbuckling her belt from her pants.

I was stunned by the thought. I didn't know if I had another one in me but I sure was going to try. Shit why would I let this opportunity slip by?

Officer Lopez unzipped her pants officially telling me that it was about to go down. I took one step to assist her with her clothing. I went to take off her bra and she slaps my hands down.

"We don't have a lot of time for all of that mister."

"Well, what do you want me to do," I questioned not knowing what she had wanted.

"I want you to exchange the favor and maybe you can have the whole thing soon," she answered stepping out of her pants.

I stood still for a moment taking in her words. I wasn't feeling like the dominant sex at the moment but her sexy olive skin lured me in.

I gently tug at her purple pink and black panties until I slid them down to her ankles. Her skin felt as smooth as silk. I was surprised to see that she has a tattoo from her hip down to her ankle. She stepped out of the panties and kick them towards the door. I planted both of my hands on top of her thighs and massage them firmly. She reached down and began to play with herself. Now on both knees I was at eye view of this pleasure she was giving herself. I take two of my fingers forming the perfect 'V' and dive in. I kept my tongue on her clit not moving away from it. I felt it become swollen which caused me to flick my tongue faster with the thought of me pleasing her. She began to shift her hips in a swing motion enjoying my tongue. The thought of out doing her crossed my mine. So I threw her left leg across my shoulder and gave myself a better position to make her have multiple orgasms. I felt her juice squirt hitting me on the chin. I tried to move my head to finish up this quick sex session but she grabbed the back of my wanting more. I worked my tongue rapidly and she took her leg down trying to run away. I held tight on her ass and continued to work until she'd let out a loud scream.

I jumped up not knowing what to expect. Did she like what I did? Was she going to say that I forced myself on her? Did anybody hear us?

She caught herself. Feeling ashamed shed' rushed to get dress.

"What's wrong?" I questioned knowingly. I pulled up my pants up but I wanted to dick her down now. Feeling how wet she is with my tongue only fucked with my imagination.

"I... I shouldn't have done this," she stuttered nervously.

"It's cool," I assured her holding her hand.

"I can get in a lot of trouble Maurice," she said, rushing to straighten her hair.

"Maurice? So you do know my full name?" I asked. I studied her face but all she could do was blush.

I got her.

"Yes. I read your folder. Now..." she confessed, smiling hard showing her pretty white teeth.

I cut her off "Now what?"

"You have to keep this our little secret," she said, kissing me seductively.

"That won't be a problem but what will be a problem is just this one time lesson."

"Trust me we will have many more times to get together," she said turning the knob of the closet door.

"Before you leave, why don't you tell me your name."

"My name is Jessica," she answered, taking a step out.

"Jessica. Well Jessica I will see you later on," I said slapping her on the ass.

"You sure will."

Chapter 8

The institution was still on lockdown but we were able to move about on our own. Juan and I decided to run off to work a few minutes earlier than normal. He wanted to check up on his phone call he made yesterday. I was all for it because I needed to get some money to Diana as soon as possible.

I threw some bags of laundry inside of the machines and the correct amount of soap powder. Juan was ready to make the call after rushing to prepare some clothes for the new inmates that where arriving sometime today.

I walked around the laundry room and not a guard was in sight. I only wished that Officer Lopez was working her shift with us again. I struggled to sleep thinking about fucking her. If Juan wasn't in the room I would have masturbated to the thought of fucking her. I know that I was going to get it but when was the question.

I took out the phone and ordered for Juan to make the call in the closet and I will be on the lookout. He rushed off heading for the closet. Suddenly Demarco and the rest of the workers entered with Officer Lopez. I felt like today was going to be a good day.

"Inmate are you in here alone?" Officer Lopez asked.

"No. Juan is cleaning up in the back," I answered.

Officer Lopez then began to walk around. With her black latex gloves she started to check the machines, under tables, in laundry baskets, and then she started for the back. I knew she would catch Juan handling business on the phone so I had to think quickly. I rushed over to the laundry detergent and knocked over the bottle causing it to spill over the floor.

"Inmate White!"

"I got it. I got it."

I hurried towards the storage closet. Juan was stepping out right on time.

"Maurice," Juan said to get my attention.

"Give me the phone."

"Here you go. Is everything alright?" Juan asked hesitating to walk away.

I quickly forced the phone in my pocket and rushed inside of the closet to get the mop and the bucket. "The guard on duty is looking for you. Just go back out front and let her know that you are here so she can do attendance."

"Sure."

I was moving so fast that I had forgotten to close the door behind me. I rushed back over to the spill and begun to mop up the blue liquid on the floor. Officer Lopez asked Juan a few questions in Spanish and they both laughed. I wanted to know what she had said to him. Lopez looked over at me and then walked back to the back to finish conducting her search. I didn't know if she was just playing things off or was really trying to find something in here. I hoped that Juan didn't mention the phone to her.

Officer Lopez slowly turned the corner starring me down. She wasn't as important as this information that I needed to hear from Juan.

Lopez was out of sight. Juan had informed me that he had his people mail the package overnight so I hurried to go make the phone call to B. Damn Lopez was back there snooping. I know that I had to make the call but doing it out here behind the machines was too reckless.

I snuck off again taking the mop and bucket into the storage closet. I noticed that someone had shut the closet door and maybe it was Lopez. I looked around for her and she wasn't anywhere in sight. This was the perfect time to make my important phone call.

Violently I opened the stored door and to my surprise Officer Lopez stood wearing nothing but her birthday suit. She waved me in. I dropped the mop outside of the door and darted inside of the closet. I quietly closed the door behind me and charged for her. She didn't waste a second pulling my clothes off to match her. While she was tearing my clothes off, I was gently placing kisses over her body and giving her a body search with my hands.

Finally I was totally naked and she went back down on me. I didn't want to be tricked again with just oral sex so I pulled her up by her arms. Soon as she was standing straight up, I dove in and begun to suck on her breasts. My fingers trickled down her body to her candy shop. I played with the pussy perfectly. She was moaning and becoming more wet with each stroke. Without any sign of stopping what I was doing, I quit and skillfully turned her around. I bent her over with one hand and guide my dick with the other. She moved away stopping me from going inside her.

"Here!" She said pulling out a condom from her uniform pants.

"I like the way you are thinking," I chuckled.

"Shut up and fuck me!" Officer Lopez ordered going back into position.

Officer Lopez had a nice round ass and breasts to match. I placed my hands on her waist and eased my way in. Although I had on a condom it was thin enough to feel the wetness and her lips as I pushed inside. Her pussy lips hugged my dick like her lips did yesterday. Jessica's face said it all. As I inched in deeper her face screwed up with pain. I began to thrust faster after a few strokes of gentle strokes. She placed her hands up against the wall and took in all of the pain. I held her mouth with one hand and her ass with the other. Surprisingly she threw her ass back taking all of me. Her hair was flying all over the place. I decided to give her a real test if she could take the dick. I flipped her around and made her wrap her legs around my waist. I held her up and fucked the shit out of her. Her breasts bounced up and down with each stroke. Officer Lopez rode this dick like a true cowgirl. She was screaming loud enough for anybody to hear but nobody bothered us. The harder I thrusted inside of her the more shit she'd talked. I felt her nails dig into my skin and then her pussy tensed up. Her nectar flowed down my balls like a river. I knew that she had came because she was done talking shit and all of her energy had departed. Before I could come she climbed off my dick and pulled the condom off skillfully.

"Where do you want it baby?"

"Umm..."

"Choose wisely. You can put it in my ass or my mouth. Which do you want?" She asked, continuing to stroke my shaft.

"Shit I already know what that head game is about."

"So you want to put it in my ass?"

"Nah. I want you to give me something I want forget. Suck this muthafucka like you won't ever get a chance to suck it again."

Without any questions, that's exactly what she did. She sucked me better than she'd ever did. My shaft felt like it belonged in her mouth. Officer Lopez rolled her tongue perfectly across the tip of my dick cleaning all of my juice off.

"Give me a moment," I said, getting dress and walking out. I needed a break from this woman's tongue.

"Where are you going?" She questioned, picking up her bra and covering her chest.

"Just wait right here," I ordered closing the door behind me.

I rushed off to get a new towel for her to clean off with. We had plenty of new shit.

I pulled the door open and she was right where I had left her. She was happy that I thought to get her the towel. She'd wiped her vagina and pulled her pants up.

"Here's something to remind of me," Officer Lopez said, handing me her panties.

I didn't know if I should've kept them or throw them away. I couldn't risk the guards hitting my cell and finding some panties. I would be questioned about them until I my release date. Not wanting to be disrespectful or seem unappreciative I went ahead and accepted her gift.

Buzz! Buzz! My pocket vibrated.

"What's that?" Officer Lopez questioned with a concern look on her face.

Damn I had the phone in my pocket. I hoped she'd wouldn't flip the script on me.

"It's my cell phone," I whispered.

"Cell phone? Boy you are too much."

"You're not going to take it are you?" I asked getting ready to hand it over.

"I don't know that you have a cell phone. You and I will keep this our secret along with everything else."

"Okay."

"Reese but when I want you, don't be playing any games," she said walking out.

I gave her a slap on her ass and she just looked back smiling. I closed the door behind her and waited a moment so it wouldn't look suspicious. I pulled out her panties and stuffed them in my draws.

I made my call to B anticipating to hear the good news. I was always excited when I got on with some dope and this time wasn't any different.

B answered on the first ring. He was waiting for my call. He didn't waste any time telling me how thankful he was. B was surprise and scared at the same damn time when the package came through. He told me that Sky opened the door with a puzzled look on her on her face. B said that the delivery man looked like an undercover cop. Everybody looked like a cop to him after what happened to us.

"So have you busted it open?"

"Yeah the shit is right. I have to admit that its probably better than J's shit," B said.

"Word?"

"Word family. I went in the kitchen and broke it down and the shit was right. I mean it was right!"

"That's good," I said.

"I ain't never seen some dope with a stamp on it. This muthafucka has a gorilla on it looking mean as hell."

"I need you to move that shit fast for me," I stated strongly through the phone.

"Fam that shit is gone!" B said excitedly.

"Gone?" I asked amazed.

"Yeah I got rid of it ten minutes after the delivery truck pulled off." B answered.

"So all of it is gone?" I asked.

"Yeah Reese! Gone. I don't sit on shit. It was only a whole one."

"Right. But you have to look out for Diana man. That was the whole purpose of getting it to you."

"Reese come on now. I just got out of the joint and I have to get myself a few things. Shit ain't cheap out here man."

"So you are telling me that you fucked up the bread already?" I asked feeling my temperature rising.

"Man I need some shit. I want to buy a new car and maybe get an apartment for myself."

"I can get you more but I need every last dollar sent over to her."

"Well if you can send more than do it. I will give her all of that money," B said.

"Man you must think I am stupid. Why would I send you more when you had fucked up the first one? You must be crazy!"

"Look Reese, I will shoot her a few dollars."

"What's a few dollars?" I asked waiting to hear his response.

"I will give her four bands. Shit I just spent on her and Rico a few days ago shit."

"That's fucked up B. I wouldn't have done your girl like that," I responded.

"Man fuck that bitch!" B said aggressively.

"This is not about Ashley. You are missing the point. You know what, fuck it. Give Dina that four."

"You are still going to send me some more?" B asked.

"Yeah I got you. Just make sure that you get Diana together." I said ending the call. I wasn't planning on giving him shit else after he played my girl. He was greedy as fuck. All he was worried about was looking good and maintaining his reputation.

After talking with B I was furious. I didn't want to show my emotion over the telephone because I couldn't afford him not looking out for Diana. He was going to get the picture after he see that there wasn't any gorilla packages coming through the mail. B fucked up a good thing already. I couldn't afford to give him multiple chance when it was a must to get money in here and on the streets.

I rapidly walked back to the front of the laundry room. Officer Lopez patrolled us watching our every move. I became irritated with the thought of her faking like she was a good cop. She must have noticed my looks and looked at me confused. She waited for us to be alone before she stepped to me.

"Are you upset with me?" She asked.

"Am I suppose to be happy."

"You should be."

I took a deep breath and thought about my words before I opened my mouth, "I have a lot going on in here."

"Like what? Are you in trouble?" She asked concerned.

"Don't worry about it. I can handle it," I replied.

"Just let me know how I can help you Maurice. I won't let anybody hurt you in here best believe that," she said, licking her lips.

Juan came around noticing how close we were and shuffled his feet backwards. Jessica looked behind her and noticed Juan catching in on our conversation. She quickly twisted her face up.

"Inmate White get back to work!"

I went along with her demands and started washing loads of clothes. I was amused by her acting skills.

Juan walked over to me and was concern. He thought that she had found the phone and I was going down. I assured him that I was in good hands and whispered that we would finish up this conversation back in the cell.

Chapter 9

Juan and I were in the cell talking for hours as usual. Tonight he was doing more talking than I was because I had a lot of things on my mind. I had to figure out how I was going to keep money in here rolling. Without RJ and Slick most of the white-boys wasn't going to budge without a fight. I wasn't afraid to box with anybody but I wasn't about to get into any unnecessary drama when I was going to be up for parole soon. Although I was doing some dirt in here I was smart about mine. I wasn't going to take the fall for shit and even if they'd caught me red handed then they would have to prove it.

While Juan was talking to me about baseball back at his home in Venezuela, I tuned him out. My mind wondered off thinking about Officer Lopez's words. I know that she was feeling for me and after fucking her good earlier today I knew I had her body. Now I needed her mind. Fucking her was cool but it wasn't going to get me paid in here. I had to use her and her position for what is was.

"Reese, are you sleep my friend?" Juan asked interrupting my thoughts.

"No man. I am just doing some thinking."

"What's on your mind?"

"What ain't?"

"Did you receive my gift?"

"Yes my people got it man."

"You don't sound too happy about it. I will have my men deliver another next week."

"I really appreciate that Juan but I can't allow you to do that."

"It's not a problem for me. Seriously!"

"Juan my friends aren't as loyal as yours. The people that I had you send the package to fucked it up already. He sold it already but didn't give my wife and kid shit!"

"Damn chamo! What kind of friend is that?"

"Exactly!"

Buzz!

The lock to our door became undone. Damn was this another search? Was Jessica still craving what she had earlier? My mind raced with thoughts. I looked up and I am blinded by a bright light. I knew it was a guard but who?

"Inmate White wake up!"

The voice was all too familiar. It was Officer Thurman.

"What's up?"

"I have to make this quick. I have some information for you."

I sat up in the bed planting my feet on the floor.

"Normally I would ask for a little compensation but this is a problem for the both of us. You handle this for me and I will forget the debt you owe me."

"What's this problem you're talking about?

"Your friend Ronald Jenkins wasn't killed by the Mexicans."

"Well who the fuck did it Thurman!" I barked.

"It was Steven." He answered simply.

"Who the fuck is Steven!"

"Keep your fucking voice down." Thurman whispered.

"You come in here telling me my friend is dead and not only that he wasn't killed by the muthafuckas that did it."

"You are not listening. Slick killed RJ."

"What the fuck?"

"Slick is spilling his guts about everyone even you and I. If they start investigating his allegations we all would be up shit creek."

"Wow!" Juan uttered.

"Dirty muthafucka!"

"Reese you need to handle this."

"What can I do and he's in protective custody?"

"I work the block all this week. He needs to have an accident if you know what I am saying."

"Man I don't believe this shit!"

"Get yourself together. We all can be in deep shit if the shit hits the fan."

"I will handle it."

"Now give me something," Thurman said searching the room.

"Give you something?"

"Give me that extra blanket you have."

Thurman left out with my blanket and a few books that I was intending to read. Those books probably had been in here since I first stepped foot in here. Thurman was smart but sneaky as fuck. I couldn't understand how Deion kept him on a short leash.

Taking those items wasn't nothing to me. I guess he had to play it off for a reason why he was in my room for so long. He didn't want his fellow officers to become suspicious.

When the door closed, I laid back and replayed everything in my head. I wondered why did Slick kill RJ. I had to find out before anyone else fell because of his ass. Knowing Slick it had to be for money. Regardless Slick had to go or be taught a serious lesson. I had to figure out how I would get someone to do the job without any money or power.

"Juan I want to take you up on that offer," I said quietly.

"What's that Reese?"

"I am going to need some money in here to fully keep you protected. Shit is getting real in here."

"I've told you that I don't have any money on the street but access to whatever else you need."

"I need to get another package but this time I will get my hands on it."

"How will you do that?"

"I have a special friend that will get it right in here."

"I know who you are talking about. From the way she'd looked at you, I know that you will be able to accomplish that."

"Make your call tomorrow. It's time for me to go back to work."

Chapter 10

Diana

Ring! Ring! My cell phone chimed. I rolled over and it was time for me to take Rico to school. I climbed out of bed and quickly put on a bra before Rico saw me. He was always up and ready before I was like a grown man.

I quickly got dressed and went to his room that my mother had just for him. As I walked down the hallway, I can hear my mother talking to someone. I'd peeked inside her room being careful that I didn't make a noise. She was laying on my father's old side of the bed just the talking. I listened closely and figured she was either talking to my father or God. I allowed her to continue to talk. Disturbing her wasn't an option. I planned on zooming Rico to school then coming right back. Mom had a doctor's appointment in a couple hours and I had to take her there. I could only pray for some good news.

I had went out and leased a new Chevy Impala with some of the money I had saved up from my renters. I was tired of feeling embarrassed every time I would meet up with Ashley or former co-workers. It wasn't my dream car but it was something that I could afford with my tight income. I just felt a whole lot better riding in something brand new compared to something that was old as dirt.

On the way to school, Rico only wanted to listen to rap and R & B music. He would quickly climb in and find a local hiphop radio station before I could turn on whatever I was feeling that day. He turned on a song from his tablet featuring Jason D.B.K.S. one of his favorite artists. At his young age he knew more about hiphop than I did. Of course his music had to be censored or he wasn't going to listen to it. I was just happy that I didn't have to drive far away because his school was really close to my mother's home.

While driving Rico to school my phone went off. It continued to ring until I had pulled in front of his school. I couldn't stand folks driving and talking on their phone so I refused to do it unless I had my Bluetooth audio connected through my speakers. I wasn't able to connect because by the time I had gotten ready to connect my phone to the car I would receive another call.

I thought that maybe it was the doctors calling or worse it may be something wrong with my mom. I quickly took the phone out from my purse and searched through my missed call log. Nope it wasn't anyone important. The calls came from B. I wondered what might he want and what was so damn important to be calling me so much.

After I kissed Rico on the cheek and allowed him to run off into the line of students, I placed my call. B answered with music blasting in the background like he was at a Future concert. I waited until he had turned the music down before I had said another word. I wasn't going to be cooperating in a shouting match just to talk to this man.

"Diana, it's not too early is it?"

"Too early? Too early for what?" I questioned not knowing his intentions.

"Is it too early for me to come over?"

"What do you need to come over for B?"

"I have to give you something from Reese. He urged that I made sure that you had gotten this today." He answered.

"Well I am out at this present moment. I had to take lil man to school."

"Oh, I almost forgot about that. Well I can meet you out in traffic."

"No. No. No. I can't meet you nowhere looking like this."

"Looking like what? Diana you know that you stay looking fine."

"Ugh. My hair ain't done and I have on some my night clothes."

"Diana I bet you are looking great. Let's just meet up real quick somewhere."

"Well, okay. Let's meet at the gas station near my old house. I can be there in like ten minutes."

"Alright, I'll meet you in a few."

B had me waiting for over twenty minutes until he had pulled up. I was so pissed because I knew that my mom's appointment was less than an hour away. I hope whatever Reese had to give me was very important. B parked his car and rolled the window down allowing a cloud of smoke to escape. B climbed out of a brand new Ohio State colored Camaro and he was looking like money. He wore expensive clothes and a shinny gold chain. Damn did he have some money saved up that he didn't tell anybody.

B strolled over to the passenger door and climbed in taking a seat. He gave me a hug and then just starred at me. I noticed that he had a designer book bag in his lap. He didn't say a word and stuck his hand inside of the bag and took out a few stacks of cash. Not even counting the money he handed the money over to me. I haven't held this much money since Reese was out.

"Thanks B. I so much needed this. People don't know how hard it is to raise a son alone and take care of an ill mother," I said giving B a hug.

"It was nothing. I told you that I was going to help you."

"You are a really good friend B. Reese should be proud to call you a friend."

B opened the door. "I have one more thing for you. This is why I was running a little late."

"More?"

B reached inside of his car and gave me a bouquet of assorted flowers. I wasn't going to be rude and not take them. I loved flowers. Flowers reminded me of how beautiful the world was.

"Thank you B. I really appreciate it."

"I just wanted to make you smile."

"How thoughtful. Well I have to go."

"I do to. Diana don't forget to call me if you need anything."

"I sure will," I said driving off.

When I arrived at the house my mother was looking like she was ready to go to church instead of going to the doctor's office. I looked at her and imagine being her age. I wondered how Reese and I would be.

"Those are nice flowers honey," my mom said pointing at the bouquet.

"Yes they are. A friend gave them to me," I answered smelling the flowers.

"I hope that this friend knows that you are a happily married woman. The devil will come and test your heart baby bearing all sorts of gifts."

"Mom it's not like that. He's a good guy. In fact he's one of Maurice's friends."

"Listen to your mother child."

"Yes ma'am."

During the drive my mom sat quiet and gazed out of the window in her own thoughts. I only hoped that she was actually feeling good and the doctor would tell us something good today. The medicine had my mother talking about death and preparing me for her departure. I didn't want to hear it.

We waited patiently in the waiting-room. I tried to gather my thoughts but my mother was talking so loud that the nurse at the desk had to close the sliding glass door. My mother talked to other patients like nothing was on her mind. She laughed and talked to these people like she had known them all of her life. Finally we were called to the back.

An Asian nurse asked my mom questions about her diet, pain, and bowel movements. Mom had to answer these questions every time. My mom stated that she had been having a lot of chest pain, dizziness, and shortness of breath. The nurse noted everything on her computer. She asked that my mom step out and get weighed. They had went out and came back about a minute later. The nurse added that information. Next the nurse took my mom's blood pressure and noted that. She told us that the doctor would be in shortly and left out of the room.

The short doctor entered into the room with a smile. He asked how were we and we'd answered. He took a seat and read over the notes that the nurse had on the computer. He wrote something down in a tan folder which I believed was a physical chart. Finally he took the stethoscope and asked for her to take deep breaths. The doctor couldn't hide his concern which was written all over his face. The doctor told my mother that he needed to take some blood for her and he would return later.

The doctor had his nurses draw blood from her and they had ran some tests. After the nurse drew the blood she said he would let the doctor know that we were ready for his return.

When he had entered, he said that the test results wouldn't be available for a couple of days or so. He wanted to admit her to the nearest hospital to do further testing. He said that he didn't like my mom's symptoms and feared that she was getting worse. I had to agree with admitting her. My mother didn't want to go back to the hospital that was near her house because that was the hospital my father died in. The doctor had to promise that she wouldn't die there before she'd agreed to admit herself. I was talking to the doctor about taking my mom to the hospital later today after Rico had gotten out of school but he insisted that they take her from the doctor's office. That's the first time I saw fear in my mother's eyes.

I felt alone driving home. I caught myself gazing out of the window remembering my mother when I was young. She was such a beautiful woman. My mother was the ideal woman and Christian wife. She took care of the house while my father was away for work and stayed on my sister and my butt when we were in school. She supported my father when he was laid off of work and believed in his dream when he said that he was going to start up his own construction business. I wanted to be just like my mother. I was going to be that good wife and a mother for my son. I was going to hold my husband down no matter what.

Chapter 11

Reese

After work I met with some of the fellas on the yard to tell the new information about Slick. I didn't know how they would take it but something had to be done to him. If we didn't fix our problem we would look weak and become a target. It was already bad that we had to find some new muscle in here to intimidate some people. I had some candidates in mind but nothing to offer. I had to fix these problems fast but first I had to handle Slick's ass.

This new kid Smurf was known to be violent with his hands but wasn't a sure thing to do a grown man's job by bodyin' a fool. I came to the conclusion that we were going to do like how the Mexican's did us and outsource some help. I was going to pay one of the big white-boys to make sure that Slick wouldn't say shit to anyone else again. I knew that it was going to cost me more than I had to offer. I was going to need help with this payment and establishing a plan.

Demarco, Ed, and myself discussed the matter again amongst ourselves after I had broke the news to everyone we fucked with. No one was surprised that Slick was a snake. Demarco was ready to put out the word but I had to remind him that we couldn't even cross the mind of being involved. Demarco wanted to know what I had in mind so I had told him my idea. Both of them was with it. In fact Demarco volunteered to assist with some funds. We all came up with the plan of having someone on the inside put something in Slick's food. We all new that Slick was a diabetic and ate differently from us. All someone had do from the kitchen in which most of the white boys ran was to put something in his food to cause him to have a reaction. He would know that it was a warning from us but the kitchen would only be looked as making a mistake.

Simple and clean.

The fellas and I went down to evening chow together with the plan stuck in our minds. Ed was going to somehow ask the cooks to do this job for us. We had cash on us and plenty of weapons just in case they had acted nuts.

I was standing directly behind Ed as we were served our portions. Ed was searching the chow hall frantically for something. Demarco must have sensed it and looked back at us and I signaled back telling him that I didn't know when Ed was going to make his move.

Suddenly Ed grabbed his juice drink and walked over with his food to the all white table. We looked at him like he was crazy but maybe he was. I thought that he was going to whisper to one of the servers for them to pass along the word but he had his own plans.

We sat studying the whole sea of white men as we ate our food. Ed's dark ass stuck out like a sore thumb. He wasn't paying us any mind as he talked to a high ranking white inmate. I continued to keep my eyes on them and they kept their attention on us.

When it was time to go, Ed rushed to get back over to us. He was looking lost so I couldn't read his face.

"Ed what's up?" Demarco questioned.

"It's on."

"That's what I am talking about man," I cheered.

"He said that everything would go down tomorrow."

"That fast!" I asked.

"Yeah."

"Slick is going to get his. RJ was a good dude."

"Yeah he was," I said walking towards the cell block.

"Payback is a bitch," Demarco added.

I had went to work and again Officer Lopez was working the laundry room. I believed she wanted some more action but my big head was thinking today. I needed her to pass this note to Thurman because he was in the medical block and I wanted to inform him on the plan. He had to make sure that Slick had received the correct tray or the plan would fail.

I meet Jessica in the storage closet. She went ahead of me. When I entered she was slowly pulling down her pants. My manhood stood straight up but I had to get myself together. I pulled out the letter which was tucked away in my draws. Her eyes got big believing that I was about to whip it out but she was quickly disappointed when I kept him inside of my pants. Her mouth dropped. I stepped to her and grabbed two fist full of ass and told her without any fear in my voice that she had to do this for me. She went to open the letter and I snatched it out of her hand and stuffed it in her chest pocket. I walked out without saying a word and went back to my duties.

Officer Lopez continued to do her job. She wasn't giving me much eye contact but I had a lot of faith in her that she was going to pass along the note. Demarco took notice at both of our actions and knew that I pushed the letter on her. He was on edge waiting for everything to take place also. This was something we had to do.

The next morning I was on the edge of my seat in the chow hall waiting for Ed to walk back over there to the white guys. Ed sat with them eating his cereal and boiled eggs. Yellow boiled egg yolk hung on the bottom of his lip as he talked to them. He was frowning and shaking his head like they were telling him something bad. Demarco and I watched Ed like a hawk as he talked.

After Ed's conversation with them he told us that the kitchen cooked did his job this morning.

Officer Lopez came to my cell and escorted me to the laundry saying that I had some officer uniforms to clean. I hated working for them but it was part of the job. I thought that she was trying to pull her rank on me. Wanted to enforce her power on me so I could be a model inmate and do what I was told.

Lopez showed me the dirty uniforms and walked away. I assumed my job cleaning the officer clothing. I noticed a piece of paper on the first uniform. It was a note from Thurman. He didn't put his name on it but I knew it was from him. The noted stated that the threat was noted. Slick didn't have a just an allergic reaction to the food he was poisoned. The cooked blended up a gang of apple seeds and put it in Slick's apple sauce. Apple seeds have a small percentage of cyanide which is a poison. The cook also cooked his fish sticks in peanut oil which Slick was allergic to.

After Slick ate his lunch he was having trouble breathing. The nurses figured that he had an allergic reaction but didn't know that cyanide was in his system. They rushed him to the hospital where he was treated.

I was happy about the news. I ripped up the note and tossed it in the trash. I felt a sense of relief come over me. I rushed over to the uniforms and cleaned them like a professional dry cleaning store. I even decided to thank Officer Lopez for her hard work with some hard dick.

Chapter 12

Diana

Church was always good for my mind and soul. With so much going on in my life I needed to the hear "the word." I had been staying away from the church for over three years because a lot of my fellow members and pastor witnessed my husband being drug out of our wedding in handcuffs. I wasn't in the mood to hear the noise about my husband or nosey members asking about the welfare of my mother so I strayed away. I decided against my emotions and risk of embarrassment and went with my heart. I had to go to church and receive some healing.

With Rico in the back and my Gospel music blasting I was ready for a joyous time with fellowship and a place to worship. I turned the ignition and I was interrupted by a call. I noticed that the call was from the hospital. I figured that it was my mom calling to talk about the Bible since she couldn't attend church. I answered.

A nurse with a soft voice told me on the other end of the phone call to notify me that my mother has fell down trying to walk around the hallways. My jaw dropped with the thought of my mother in pain from her injuries. She urged that I come to the hospital as fast as I could. I didn't hesitate to turn the car around screeching the tires in the direction for hospital.

I drove rapidly through the streets to get to the hospital. I parked my car in front of the hospital and left it next to an ambulance. Rico and I rushed through the hospital. We decided to take the stairs to the third floor instead of waiting for the elevator to come down. When we reached my mom's floor I was out of breath and Rico just smiled and kept running.

We entered my mom's room and she was on more machines than when I left. The doctor took his eyes away from my mother and asked to speak with me away from Rico. We stepped closer towards the door.

He whispered, "Your mom had another heart attack."

"How could that happen? Where were y'all at?"

"Your mother walked around to the room your father died in and she fainted. Our nurses brought her back to the room and we did all we could."

"Did all you could? What does that mean doctor?" I cried knowing his response but I wasn't prepared to hear his words.

"We will see how everything goes through the night but it might be best if you were to put her in Hospice care."

"Hospice?" I cried.

A nurse rushed out of a near bye room and hugged me. The doctor continued to talk mute my ears. All I could do was cry like a baby.

They'd settled my mother in her room in the Hospice hospital. She knew about her surroundings and was ready for whatever God had in stored for her. I continued to pray for my mother but I watched her for nine days get worse.

My mother heard me praying and took the breathing machine away from her face to talk to me. I watched her struggle to lift the bed up using the remote so I rushed to her bedside.

"Diana, you have been a blessing to us all. You are a special woman. I am proud of the wife, mother and daughter which you have become. I need you to continue to do as such and not worry about me. I am going to see the king and be in his mansion with your father."

"Momma don't talk like that. You have a long life to live," I cried holding her hand.

"Baby, I am ready to leave this world behind. I'd enjoyed it will I was her for 68 years. Life has given me a lot and…" My mom said stopping to cough.

"Are you okay? Should I get the doctor?"

"No I am fine. You go home and love my grandbaby."

"I will momma."

"I love you Diana…" She coughed again.

"Let me get somebody momma. I will be right back."

I let go of my mother's hand and took a long look at her before I went for the nurse's station. She wasn't moving and I noticed her mouth wide open. Tears blurred my vision but I did hear the monitors going off. I lost her right in my hands. My mother was gone and I was in this world all alone.

Inside of the car, I hesitated to call Reese. He was my best friend and husband. It only sucked that I could only talked to him for five or so minutes a day and sometimes those days are far between. Tonight I needed him. Not physically but as a friend that will just listen to my heart ache. I needed him here with me.

I pulled out my cell phone and called him but I didn't receive an answer. I tried again two or three minutes later and I got the same result. The voicemail kept picking up. Putting the phone back inside of my purse my phone suddenly rings. I pulled it back out expecting to see Reese prison number on the caller identification but it wasn't him. It was B.

Reluctantly I didn't answer B's call. I wasn't in any position to talk to B about his mess or about anything else. I had big problems.

With Rico over my sister's house I had to face the music and tell her that our mother had passed. That wasn't going to be as difficult as telling Rico. Rico and my mother really grew tight since we had to move in with her. I had to think about his feelings. He had been through so much at such an early age. He lost Reese to prison, Christian to the streets, my father, and now my mother. I knew his little heart would be destroyed. How much more could the boy take?

Driving a few city blocks, I did come up with idea for B to get Rico for the night so I can figure out how I was going to explain the passing of his grandmother. This would also give me some time to be with my sister and comfort her.

I called B. He listened to my pain and assured me that he would play a larger part in Rico's life until Reese came home. He said that he would take Rico out to eat and buy him some video games for his game system. I thought that would be a great idea.

B came over right away to pick Rico up. B was happy to get Rico for the night. He picked Rico up of his feet and told him of their plans for the night which made Rico so happy. I felt good seeing the joy on his face.

Rico gave me a kiss and ran off to B's car. B assured me that things will be okay and he will do his part with helping me. His actions were speaking and I had noticed. Every time I needed help B was there. He was turning out to be a really good friend for my family.

B hugged me and gave me a soft kiss on the cheek. He walked off throwing Rico's book bag filled with Rico's clothes over his back. I watched as they'd until walked to the car. I noticed a pretty female get out from the passenger's seat. She gave me a fake ass smile and waved at me. I didn't bother to wave back catching the fakeness she was throwing. I wondered if this was the stripper Sky whom B had been fooling with. She opened Rico's door, walking all of the way around the car swinging her hips. She was dressed like she was about to get dropped off for the club wearing some tight jeans revealing the crack of her butt. Her butt was looking at me clear as day while she helped put Rico's seatbelt on. This woman was really trying to show off her curves believing that I was a threat towards her man.

She had life messed up.

Chapter 13

Reese

Having to pay my part of the payment for getting Slick fucked up by the white guys I came up with a master plan. I asked Officer Lopez to bring in a cell phone and a pack of New Ports. The cell phone was for Demarco since he paid the men up front and the cigs were for me to wiggle in here. She agreed to do whatever I asked of her. Officer Lopez said she stored everything in our secret bedroom and I couldn't wait to get my hands on it. I passed the word to Demarco and he was excited himself. He probably be the one who would buy the cigs since he hadn't had a real cig in many years. Demarco had to wait until we went to work until I could get my hands on the items for him. Sky had wrote me a letter promising me to make today her first visit here. I can't lie I was excited to see her.

I went into the visitation room felling like a pimp. I had everything a convict could wanted while doing time. I had pussy, food, money, envelopes, a cell phone, and respect.

Officer Thurman was working the visitation along with a couple other guards. He searched me to enter the visitation room. While he was conducting his searched I asked him to do me a favor and at some point during my visit give me a moment to be alone with my visitor. He acted like I was pulling his teeth but after a few moments of debate he said he will find away but if I was caught it was all on me and her. I accepted the agreement and walked away.

Thurman walked in behind me and relieved the guard on duty to watch over us. I found a woman bent over drinking water from the water faucet. I knew it was Sky. I could recognize her ass in a police line-up. I remember giving her a 69 in the hotel with all of that ass in my face. Her pussy tasted so good. Sky was curvy than most. Sky just had it all. Looks, smarts, good head game, and even better pussy. Sky also was a down chic. The letters and visits when I was in the county jail only brought us closer. Sky was an open bi-sexual and wasn't afraid to share. That was what I liked most.

Sky turned to me and it felt like my heart skipped a beat when I saw her face. Her face was marked with a black eye. Although the mark was bold, it didn't affect her beauty. I bet one of her patrons at the strip club tried to cop a feel and she was going for it so they did a punk move and hit her. I wished I was on the streets to handle whoever did that to her.

Sky gave me a hug and a gentle kiss. This wasn't the Sky I knew. I wondered what had changed. I know that B wasn't in her head because she wouldn't be here. I was just use to the nasty Sky. The one who would lick all over my body and damn near suck my lips off my face when we kissed.

"It's good to see you," I said gazing over her.

"It's good to see you. I see that you are getting your body right."

"I'm trying," I laughed.

"Keep it up, it looks good on you."

"So how have you been? Honestly?"

"I am doing okay. I have not been working at Keith's much."

"Why not? He should be making a lot of money."

"It's not that. I wanted to get out of the city. With B all up in the club, I can't make my money the way I would like."

"So how are you getting money?"

"My girls and I have been stripping at the club in East Columbus. It's not like Keith's but I make enough to survive."

"Your girl China lives in Columbus don't she?" I asked remembering fucking China.

"No. She lives in Cincinnati. We went up there to dance and the money started rolling in."

"Okay."

"Treasure has been up there a few times. She told me to tell you hi and her brother Lamar asks about you all of the time when she goes to visit him."

"Yeah Mar is my boy. I forgot that she lives up there."

"She's been wanting my girls and I to assist her with setting some dope boys up. You know how she get down."

"Yeah. Treasure is some shit."

"I was thinking about it but B ain't going to let me."

"Is he your man now?"

"No!"

"He acts like he is. He knows that I am in love with you."

"Was it B that did that to your face?"

"Yes."

"Damn! He's out there foolin."

"He started tripping once I told him that I was coming to see you. I didn't know he was going to put his hands on me."

"Don't worry about it I will give him a call. In the meantime I want you to pack your shit and move out."

"Move out of my own shit? Hell no! He have to leave not me. I only tolerated his shit for you Reese."

"Has he hit you before?" I asked studying her face.

She looked around the room and then back at me before speaking, "Yes. Reese he tried to rape me."

"What?"

"What do you mean what? You don't believe me?" She said raising her voice.

"I'm not saying that. You have to understand that I have been knowing B my whole life so hearing this comes as a surprise."

"I need you to do something Reese! I wouldn't be in this situation if I wasn't in love with you!" She stressed.

"I will talk to him. I know the way to get to B and that's through his pockets. If I cut him off for putting his hands on you he will stop."

"And if he tries to attack me again?"

"I will have to go another route that he won't like."

"That's all I wanted to hear."

I put my right hand on her thick thigh, "Now I want you to do something for me."

"Anything Reese," she said cheerfully.

I stare dead in her eyes making sure that she was listening. "I want you to work for me. You know the gift I mailed to you?"

"Yeah."

"From now on you get rid of half of it in the strip club. Have your girls help you. I know how the strippers like to party. If you can't push it well, then give some to B and have him eating out the palm of your hand. The other half I want you to give to this lady name Jessica. She will call you tomorrow with more instructions. You keep half of the money and the rest that you make put aside for when I get out."

"Okay. You don't want me to give your wife anything.

"No. I will make sure she's taken care of."

"You think you're getting out soon?" She asked smiling from ear to ear.

"Yes I do. My lawyer is coming to visit me next month to discuss everything he is doing for me on his behalf."

"That's great! Well I will have the girls ready to give you another night that you will never forget."

She took my hand and rub it on her pussy. I looked at her and smile. I noticed Officer Thurman walking towards us so I pulled my hand away.

"Let's do something now."

"Now? Here?" She questioned looking at me like I had lost my mind.

"I'm serious," I whispered.

"I see you are."

"Excuse me miss, I found your driver's license in the hallway. Can you please follow me," Thurman said walking towards the exit.

I watched Thurman escort Sky towards the exit and signaled for me to follow. Thurman was a smart muthafucka. I bet he had whomever in the tower watching the cameras working with him. I didn't give a fuck either way. Worst case scenario was a month or so in the hole and Sky banned from visitation.

I waited for Thurman to walk back into the visitation room before I followed behind Sky. Thurman took Sky to the restroom right next to the last door stopping us from being free. He came back in and nodded his head signaling for me to get it in.

I rapidly speed walked for the restroom door. Other inmates was wondering what in the world I was doing but they kept their mouths shut. This was my first time walking past a line that was marked only for guards or visitors better known to us as out of bounds.

The door squeaked as I gently pushed it open. I hesitated for a moment to enter into the woman's restroom but I believed that was where she was waiting for me. I stepped in and there Sky was waiting right there.

"This is crazy Reese but I love it."

"We don't have much time to do what we have to do," I said pulling my pants down to my knees.

"Now that's a man."

I chuckled at her response. She was staring down at my dick.

"Come on girl don't be scared. The guard is looking out for us but we only have a few minutes."

She didn't hesitate to pull her pants down and toss them on the counter. She pulled her panties to the side and allowed me to enter her. I felt her panties rubbing against the side of my shaft as I stroke inside of her. I was surprise to feel how tight she was. She told me through the mail how she had been using toys to keep her company until I came home but it sure didn't feel like it. I threw one of her legs up on my arm and she stood on the other. I struggled to get my dick in her with us both standing up. I picked her up and sat her on the edge of the counter and slid right in. Sky liked how I opened her legs wide open so that I could penetrate deeper inside of her. I held on her thighs and thrusted so fast that I came before she did. Sky didn't want me to stop but I didn't want to risk getting busted. I pulled out and went to pull up my pants but she'd grabbed my dick and forcefully jacked it as she kissed me. My manhood wasn't going to work being all nervous and shit. I was going soft and she noticed.

"Reese what's wrong?"

"I told you we don't have much time."

"I don't care about getting caught. I need that dick inside of me now," she begged.

I studied her body and wanted to slide back in her but I chose otherwise. I gave her a kiss on the lips and started for the door. I was glad that I did because soon as I pulled up my pants up Thurman walked in to get me. I caught him checking out Sky's curves. I nudge him and tell him that I was right behind him. Sky looked at me sadly and started to pull her pants up. She struggled to get the pants over ass. I told her that I would call her and she blew me a kiss good bye.

Outside of the door Thurman played things off and handcuffed me in front of the other inmates and visitors. He tried to handle me really rough. He made the handcuffs too tight and I was going to let him know about it. I talked shit to him like I was really mad. He took me out of the visitation room and then took the cuffs off.

"Reese, I know you had fun with that."

"It was okay. I didn't have time to get into it like I wanted to."

"I wish I had a second with a woman that fine," Thurman said shaking his head imagining having Sky.

"You can man just get your game tight."

"That's the second woman I have seen visit you in here. You are something like a ladies man huh?"

"No not really. I have my wife and a mistress. They both have their jobs and I have mine."

"Well, Officer Lopez came in here and saw you with that other woman and she wasn't quite fond of your visitor. I had came to get you because at any moment she was going to burst in there and blow up the whole scene."

"She was bugging like that?"

"Yeah man. I believe she is working the laundry room so walk on egg shells when you go to work. She might throw your ass in the whole if you just look at her wrong."

"Okay. Thanks for everything Thurman. I will send your wife a dollar soon."

"You do that."

I walked to work ready to hear what this woman had to say for herself. I was told that Latin women had a mouth on them more than black woman. Whatever she was going to say was going to go in one ear and out the other.

Demarco met me at the entrance of the door like a door-man. He opened the door and followed me in. I knew that he wanted his phone but I had some other business to take care of first before I was going to handle mines with him.

I walked over to Officer Lopez and checked in for a head count. She was trying to ignore me but I knew that she couldn't resist me. I grabbed some laundry and walked behind her brushing my dick against her ass. She looked over her shoulder and rolled her eyes. She was really mad at me about something.

"Officer Lopez can you open the back door so that I could take out the trash," I asked walking to the back.

I heard the keys jingling on her side walking behind me. I was going to get to the bottom of her attitude.

"What's wrong with you today?" I asked pulling the trash.

"Nothing," she snapped.

"Nothing hell. Something is wrong with you."

"I saw you today."

"Saw me doing what?" I wondered, walking towards another trash can.

"I saw you with that girl. I don't like her," Officer Lopez said smacking her tan thick lips.

"Sky? She's an old friend," I said blowing her off.

"A friend huh? I guess…"

I cut her off, "Guess what? Sky isn't anything to me but a friend. Her and I are really good friends. That's it and that's all."

"So why were you in the restroom with her? I bet you two weren't in there talking about the news."

"Damn! That's how you feel? Listen, yes I fucked her. The fact is I had to fuck her. She is making sure that I eat in here."

"So you fuck the bitch? Reese you are such a fucking dog!" Officer Lopez said starting for the back door.

"I have to do what I have to do in here to survive! I don't have anybody out there looking out for me!" I said dropping both of the trash bags on the floor.

"Listen poppi. I don't like the bitch! I told you before that I will help you in any way. All you have to do is ask but you have to cut her off."

"Cut her off?"

"I know that you are going to write her and maybe call her from your phone but I don't want to see her in here visiting you anymore."

"What?" I laughed at the thought of being controlled.

"This is my territory. That bitch can have everything else." Officer Lopez said firmly. She stepped directly in my face.

"If I agree to that bullshit then you will have to step up and do the shit she's willing to do."

"What's that?"

"I need to make some money in here. I want you to bring dope in here for me and I will make sure you get what you want. We both will be satisfied."

"How am I suppose to get some dope Reese?" Officer Lopez asked.

"Let me worry about that."

"No I need to know! I don't want to get caught up in any mess."

"Okay. Well Sky will give you what you need to bring in every Friday."

"Sky?"

"Yes Sky! I want you to give her a call later."

"I don't believe this shit."

"You said you want to help me. This is helping me. I will make sure that you get your piece of the pie."

"I don't want any."

"Cool, more for me."

We both laugh.

"Here's her number. Make sure that you call here as soon as possible. It's time to go to work."

"Yes it is," Officer Lopez said pulling me into the storage closet.

Chapter 14

Diana

I sat outside of B's apartment waiting for Rico to come out. I called B about thirty minutes ago informing him that I was on my way. I wasn't about to be the victim of Sky giving me any dirty looks because the way I am feeling right now I would be all over that girls face with blows. I decided to sit out here and get my thoughts together.

Although Rico was only about to turn six years old he was a very intelligent boy. He knew what was going on around him. I couldn't hide my emotions when we were out and I would see a family together and my eyes would tear up. I couldn't hide how I felt about his father each time we would talk. Reese had a way with my heart and it was hard for me to live not having him here. Each time I would tear up or breakdown, Rico new exactly what to say or do. He was a good kid. Rico would wipe my tears, make me something to drink, or simply allow me to just hold him. Breaking the news to him today about my mother was going to hurt him. There wasn't any way around it. I couldn't lie to him because he would see right through me. I never lied to him and today I wasn't going to start.

I needed a friend to talk to. I picked up the phone and tried to call Reese but like usual he didn't answer. I was getting tired of that mess. I wanted to get his perspective on telling Rico about his grandmother's passing. My sister said that I shouldn't tell him because of the circumstances with everything that had happened to him in such a little amount of time but I thought otherwise.

Rico was going to come home and run into his grandmother's room expecting to see her and she wouldn't be there. What was I going to say then? It would be best for me to take him out somewhere where I could talk to him without any interruption and allow him to vent.

Suddenly I got a call and Reese's name came on my screen. He must have known I was thinking about him for him to call me right back. I connect the Bluetooth and proceed to talk.

"Hi baby. I just tried to call you."

"Well you know that I don't be having this phone on me. I have to keep it hidden away from these police in here."

"I keep forgetting."

"Baby I have some great news for us. We are about to be right back. Shit even better than we were. You will get your car back and when I come home we will buy another house. Shit we will be living next door to one of the Bengal players or something. We about to be paid baby you hear me?" Reese rambled.

"I'm here," I responded.

"Listen my cell mate is a made man. He has more dope than he could count. When I say we are about to be rich, best believe me. He owes me and promised that when he gets out he will make sure that whatever I need he will get it. This is the type of connect I need. The fucking cops think I was doing something before, shit I'm going to be eating like a fucking boss. His name is Juan and he will be released in less than five months. I gave him your number so soon as he get out we will be good."

"Whoa, whoa, whoa. Reese slow down. You didn't ask me once how was my day. How was Rico. Nothing." I cried.

"You're right baby. I am just so excited to get our life back."

"Reese right now is not the time for that. I have been wanting to talk to you so bad. I needed you to comfort me and tell me that everything is going to be alright."

"Everything will be alright," Reese interjected.

"Reese you're not listening to me. You are so selfish! I have been dealing with so much lately."

"What's wrong baby?"

"Reese I lost my mother," I broke down crying.

"Damn, that's crazy!"

"Yeah I don't know what to do. I'm just getting over losing my dad and it's still hard that you are not physically here."

"I know baby."

"Not to mention I have to pay for the funeral expenses. My mom used most of the money she had to help with the wedding and extra bills she'd accumulated since we had moved in."

"Don't worry I have this money coming any day now. I will do my best to get you some real cash ASAP."

Reese became more sympathetic. He listened while I cried to him about my mother. His words were so soothing that I almost thought that he was sitting right next to me. The more we talked I began to feel a lot better. Reese reminded how much my mother loved God and new that she was going to a better place.

Looking down in my lap scrolling through my timeline on social media continuing to talk to Reese, I didn't even notice B standing outside of my door. I noticed B holding bags in his hands from Kids Footlocker, Children's Place, and Toys R Us. Rico also had bags in his hands along with his book bag.

"Baby can you call me back? I need to help lil man with getting in the car."

"Hi mommy!" Rico said with excitement.

"Hi baby."

"I'll meet up with y'all a little later today. I have something to give him," B said.

"Who's that?" Reese questioned.

"Boy stop it. It's B," I said simply.

I had almost forgot that I was talking to Reese.

"Babe B bought this boy all sorts of stuff. He has really been looking out for us since he has been home."

"He should. I am giving him the damn money to do it."

"Baby stop. At least he is helping. The rest of your so called friends ain't shit!"

"Diana I have to do something."

"I'm sure you do Reese," I said ending our phone conversation.

I sat my phone down on the passenger seat and climbed out to put the bags in the trunk. "Where's your girlfriend at?"

"Who Sky?" B asked, looking at me confused.

"Yes..." I said slowly.

"Um, um. Shit I don't know. I think she went to go see her man. But I like how you added that she's my girlfriend. We are not together. My bitch is my money," B said closing the trunk of the car. He chuckled as he walked me back to my door.

"See you later Uncle B!" Rico shouted.

"Yeah alright little man. I 'll see you," B replied slapping Rico's hand.

"I'm taking him to the park in my old neighborhood."

"I'll be through."

"Okay. See you later."

I decided to take Rico to a park and have some Wendy's which was his favorite fast food. Reese and I had taken Rico here a few times when he was just a baby. I had laid a cover onto the grass and placed our food on top.

"Rico mommy wants to talk to you about something," I said taking a sip of the cold strawberry lemonade.

"Okay."

"Are you listening Rico?"

"Yes mom."

"You know your grandmother was really sick?" My voice trembled.

"Yeah."

"I had to take her to the hospital and the doctor said she can't come home," I said trying hard not to tear up.

"So grandma went to Heaven?" Rico said dumping his nugget in some sauce.

"Yes baby."

"She's with grandpa then. We will see them later momma."

"Yes we will."

"Rico!"

I looked around and I saw B running towards us.

"Mom look!" Rico said jumping up and down with excitement.

B bought this boy a damn dog. Rico was spoiled by everyone. This dog would help comfort him which made me happy. Rico dropped down to his knees and wrestled with the puppy playfully. He laughed and played with the pup until we left.

Chapter 15

Reese

It's been five months since I had my first pack of dope smuggled in here. Things were going great for me in here and for my family out there. Officer Lopez continued to hold me down with the ass and killer head game. In here she was like my wife. We would argue, fuck and make-up. She had even gave me her lunch a few times so we had considered that dinner. The only thing we haven't done was introduce each other to our families. Honestly she had met mines several times when Diana visited. Diana would have killed her ass if she would have known that I was fucking her.

Everyone in the cell block decide to give Juan a going away party including some of the white inmates. Life was good behind the wall. We all bought a load of commissary and made food with what we had to chip in. The guards even took part. The guards were playing cards, another guard was doing magic tricks. We never seen the block this live without any drama.

The day wasn't going to end perfect because I got word that the guards were going to hit our block tonight. They wanted to attempt to catch us slipping but on this go around I was well prepared with people on the inside. I was told that they were hitting the institution hard because two guys passed away from some drugs. These dudes were idiots. Drawing attention to all of us because they can't handle their dope.

Juan pulled me to the side after I won a game of spades with Ed against some new inmates. Juan was smiling and he embraced me with a hug before he had spoken.

"Reese I can't begin to tell you how much I appreciate your loyalty and more importantly your friendship."

"Same to you friend."

"I will repay you and treat your family as if it were my own."

"I appreciate that. I'm sure that you are a man of your word."

Officer Thurman entered the cellblock and requested that I go to the laundry. As we walked he tells me that he knows about the dope that was being brought in and he wanted to get in. He was upset that I was using someone else within these walls other than him. He mentioned that his wife was looking forward to a luxury wedding anniversary. He believed that I was going to chip in on that vacation.

"If I were the one bringing in the dope I would be a fool not to fuck with you, Officer Thurman."

Thurman didn't say a word and took me to the laundry to get the supplies off the truck. I asked for help but these guards loved to see a black man sweat.

Surprisingly, Officer Lopez was here. She didn't work my shift earlier because she was scheduled to work the control tower. Since today was Friday normally she would be here to give me another package but today was different.

Today she was here to take out whatever I didn't sell. I had a whole ounce of dog food to get rid of and four cell phones. I couldn't risk hiding the phones in here any longer. I decided only to use a phone when she would work in the laundry. My phone calls home was far and between just as were my visits.

I gave her the dope and cell phones. I watched her shove the dope down her pants and phones into her bra. She had planned on putting the phones in her locker until her shift was over.

She knew that our meeting was strictly business so I had proceeded to unload the material and set it in the proper location.

Officer Lopez allowed me to go back to the cellblock on my own. We agreed that we didn't need to be seen always together especially with taking a risk with the dope.

The guards soon after locked us down for evening head count. Juan was aware of the search but it didn't bother him much because he was leaving in a few more hours.

Like clockwork the guards stormed in. I was prepared for anything they through at me. I was fully dressed and waited at the door like I was ready to go to work.

Juan climbed out the bed laughing at their actions. He was already smelling the fresh pine air of the near bye forests.

The guards tore up every cell in every block. To their dismay after searching the whole institution they only found about twelve boxes of cigs and a few ounces of weed. They wanted to find the dope so bad that they interrogated anyone they had suspected like they were DEA agents.

Juan and I went back in our cell and laughed as if we were at a comedy show. He was filled with so much joy. I could only imagine the last night that I would have in here. I closed my eyes and allowed my dreams to entertain me.

Chapter 16

Diana

Reese friend Juan called me last night to give me the location to meet today. I was so nervous talking to that man. The way that Reese talked about that man I thought he was the real Scareface. A Hispanic man with money, power and respect. The thought of him killing me for any mess ups or weird suspicions gave me butterflies. He informed that I could bring only one person to our meeting but that made me nervous. The only person that I knew would protect me without a doubt in my mind was B. B was all up for the idea. He hadn't been doing that well nickel and dimming quarter bricks once or twice a week.

While I was driving a rental that B got for us to down to Cincinnati, he was in the passenger seat loading two of his hand guns. He wanted to give me the third gun he had brought but I disagreed. Juan asked that we meet him at a Dominican restaurant near uptown. I didn't want to question his tactics so I agreed to the location and time.

We pulled up front of the location and I noticed that it was a lot of traffic inside. It was a nice looking place. I thought that I was going to some ran down place but this place was quite nice. The odor from the food was intriguing. I wanted to hurry to enter just off the smell alone. I turned to B and I noticed him tucking a gun in his Gucci belt and stuff another inside of a jacket he was wearing.

We entered the location and I didn't have an idea of what this man looked like. I could only go off of what I imagined. None of the men in here looked like king pin drug lords if that had a look. Everyone was well dressed and looked as if they were business owners with their suits and dresses on. A hostess escorted B and I to our table and we sat. I was nervous but not like B. He was fidgeting with the menu and the silverware.

Ten minutes after sitting down, a neatly shaved athletic built man came to the table. He wasn't dressed like the rest of the customers or restaurant staff. He wore a tight V-neck, black T-shirt with multiple gold chains. He sort of looked like the rap artists French Montana.

"Excuse me sir we are waiting for someone," B added sounding irritated.

"Are you Mrs. White?" the man said taking my hand and gently kissing it.

His island accent was so cute.

"Yes I am," I answered blushing by his actions.

"Your husband is a good friend of mine. I owe him incredibly. As a gift of my appreciation I will make sure that you will be fully taken care of."

"Are you Mr. Juan?" I asked.

"Si."

"This can't be who Reese was talking about," B interjected.

Juan didn't look like he was rich like Reese was describing but I knew how to detect if a man was who he said he was within minutes. I looked him over. His teeth were clean, white and straight. His beard was neatly trimmed showing off his razor line. His chest was sculpted not too much but enough to hint that he had either been working out or was locked up. To confirm this was the man we were here to see, was when I noticed his jewelry. His chains looked solid, diamond earrings were cut from the best stones, and I knew the value of his Rolex watch. This was the man we were here to see.

"No disrespect chamo but I am here as a favor for Reese," Juan's voice quickly changed to anger.

"Chamo? What the fuck is that? You need to speak English around here homie," B said gripping his pistol.

"B calm down," I said holding B's arm down.

"Diana maybe we should just leave," B replied getting up to his feet.

"Yes maybe you should before you do something you might regret," Juan said raising his voice.

Juan snapped his finger and it seemed like everyone got quiet. Seven men stood up wearing tailored suits. Two of them pulled out guns and walked towards us. I thought that my life was about to end.

"Damn you deep," B said, searching the room.

"Mrs. White, I was told that further communication between us would be private. Your husband only wants you to discuss things with me. No other ears are invited in our conversation."

"I'm not going anywhere!" B barked.

"B I will be fine. My husband requested for the man to talk to me in private so we will respect that," I said sounding like Reese use to when he was handling business.

B looked lost allowing my words to settle. He looked down at me making sure that I knew what I was doing and I gave him a polite smile. B maneuvered around the table and went for the exit.

"Everybody don't know how to conduct business in a civilized manner. Now shall we talk?" I said.

Juan ordered us a bottle of wine and some food. The waiter brought us a plate of La Bandera accompanied with tostones. Tostones are fried plantains. White rice, stewed beans and what I believed was a beef roast all smelled so good. It was seasoned very well and I enjoyed every bite.

I enjoyed Juan's company. Mr. Juan truly felt like Reese was a dear friend to him. We sat and ate while he told me stories of Reese. They were up nights at a time talking about me and his wife. I didn't know how much Juan and Reese had in common until he told me his story.

Before Juan had departed, he told me that the gift would be waiting for me in the kitchen. He said it would be in a large black trash bag near the rear exit. He told me that he saw why Reese stayed up at night talking about me. I smiled. Just as he was about to step away he'd promised me that I would have more gifts to come. He gave me instructions to his calling method in which he would call me every first Saturday of the month to get more product. Juan wasn't a stranger anymore no matter how B felt about the man. He politely asked to be excused from the table and he smoothly put on his sunglasses and left out of the restaurant.

B rushed back in, "So where's the shit at? I knew Reese was full of shit."

I didn't quickly answer B like he had intended me to but my ears did catch him disrespecting Reese which was a no, no.

"B you're not going to disrespect my husband like that!" I snapped walking away from the table.

I was about to go off on B but I wasn't going to give him the time of day. I was in a nice establishment and I was going to conduct myself as a boss like they assumed I was.

"I didn't mean..."

I cut him off. "B I will meet you at the car. I have to go to the little girls room."

After B excused himself again, the waiter came back and gave me what I assumed was the check. I know Juan didn't play me like that. I opened the burgundy colored folder and a note was in it. Juan left a note saying that my gift was in the kitchen like previously instructed.

"Which way to the kitchen?" I asked the waiter.

The waiter didn't say a word and signaled for me to follow him. I went along with his gesture. I followed the man into the kitchen where I was lost. I looked around for the bag and it wasn't anywhere in sight. I did find the bright red exit sign hanging in the rear of the kitchen. I walked towards the exit sign and I found a black trash bag against the door. Carefully I opened the bag making sure that it wasn't trash. Realizing that it wasn't trash, I squat down and fully opened the bag. I grabbed the first thing my eyes could see. I pulled out a brick of what I assumed was cocaine wrapped in yellow plastic with a gorilla stamped on it. I dug in again to find seven bricks. I struggled to pick the bag up but I had mind over matter. I picked the heavy bag up in heels and all and carried it through the back door around to the car. B climbed out excited to see me or the bag of gifts. He took the bag from my hands and threw it in the trunk. He couldn't resist from peeking inside before he had closed the trunk.

Driving home my only thought was not to get pulled over by one of these state boys. They were all up and down 75 it seemed. More than usual. B continued to rant about how good this would be for the streets because when Reese sent him a package it went like hot cakes. He was really familiar with the gorilla stamped dope. I wasn't familiar with nothing about the dope game.

I guess I was going to find out.

Chapter 17

Reese

It had been nine months since Juan had gotten out. Everything was going smooth with the business within these walls. Shit had been going so well that I had others running shit and I just played the background collection like a banker.

Juan had been doing right by Diana. She was back on her feet and was moving forward with becoming a boss herself. Diana was making all of the right types of moves with her money. She first bought her a car. She got something that she'd always wanted and that was a brand spanking new Porsche Panamera. Next she'd paid off her mother funeral debt. With all of this money she thought about the real estate market and bought four ran down apartments in the Five Oaks neighborhood. She put over two hundred thousand into renovating the apartments and was looking to put the apartments for rent any day now.

When Juan dropped twenty-five kilos on her she didn't get scared like a lot of mid-level dealers would, she put them in the streets. Diana used B as her right hand man against my better judgement. He even knew that I was against him working with her not because I didn't trust him but because B was only out for his self. I didn't want to wish bad luck on them but I knew if the feds ran up on him again then it was going to be ugly.

It seemed like it had happened over night how Diana went from not knowing shit about the game to becoming one of the biggest dealers in Ohio. With Juan's dope, his muscle, and her smarts she was a force to be wrecking with. The streets were calling her the 'Bird Lady.'

Money wasn't solving all of our problems especially mine. The guards started hitting us with more random searches lately. I felt things closing down on me. The benefit I had for others selling the drugs was that I wasn't under the spotlight. I barely received the dope from Officer Lopez when she brought it in. I had others getting it for me. I even changed my job and started working in the library just to do more research on how to become a writer. I would occasionally see Officer Lopez around the institution but she knew what it was. I was approaching my release date and I had to lay low.

Today I didn't have to work so I just stayed in my cell and thought about life on the streets. I couldn't wait to be on the throne with my queen and prince.

My room had been peaceful for about eight months. I had another cellmate for about a week but he was young and dumb. He wanted to prove himself by trying to act tough with other inmates and I didn't need that shit. I told him to check out or I was going to really see how tough he claimed he was. After that, I paid Thurman some petty cash to keep my cell to myself.

Suddenly I get a knock on the door. I noticed Officer Thurman standing outside of the door. He allowed himself in. He had a stack full of mail and passed me my mail. I shuffled through the mail and stopped when I saw a letter from Sky. Thurman found the exit.

Sky and I hadn't been talking much and she'd slowed down with the letters. I hadn't received a letter from her in a while. Officer Lopez put a stop to our visits. It's been too long that we haven't communicated. I needed to hear some freaky shit from her ass. She kept my mind filled with dirty fantasies of having sex with her and her friends.

Before I had opened the letter I had placed the letter against the tip of my nose searching for her sweet perfume scent. I couldn't smell a thing. This was unlike her. No perfume. No pictures. No lipstick kisses over the letter.

I opened the letter and begun to read. The letter started off good about how life had been since I had gotten her the new job. She told me that she had to quit stripping at the strip club because she'd found out that she was pregnant.

Damn did B get her knocked up?

I continued to read.

Sky said that it was hard talking to me over the phone about business when she had so much to say to me about life. Sky said that after our quick sex session in the visitation restroom that she waited for her next menstrual cycle and it never came. She didn't want to believe it knowing that she couldn't have the life with me that she'd dreamed of. It took her friend China to take her to the doctor to take an official test. The doctor gave her the same news but the math added up to us having sex. Shit hit the fan when she said that I was the father.

I was flabbergasted. I really didn't know if should've called her or write back. The thought about her hiding this from me all of this time was very upsetting. My stomach began to ache. I sighed heavily not knowing what would Diana think or do. The whole idea had my mind racing.

I sat back in the bed and read over the letter again and I realized that the baby would be born any day now. The previous thoughts I was having about my freedom were quickly fading. I was going to be in a lot of bullshit as soon as I got a breath of fresh air.

How could I be so careless?

At the end of the letter Sky said that she had about $100,000 waiting for me. She said that she was done working with Officer Lopez because she was asking too many questions about the pregnancy and dope. Sky felt as if it wasn't none of her fucking business to know who she was pregnant by. What had my antennas up was that Officer Lopez was asking about the product. She wanted to know too much.

My thoughts begun to get the best of me. I decided to get a little work out in to blow off some steam. Not five minutes into my workout I was bothered about business.

Some of the guys were wondering when the package would come in today. I didn't have an answer for them since I wasn't the one receiving the packages from Officer Lopez anymore. They told me that Officer Lopez told them that she wanted to meet me to give me the product directly. She claimed she was becoming paranoid about other officers snooping around her. Shit was becoming strange about her.

I felt something in the air like something wasn't right about Officer Lopez. I continued to walk to the laundry although I had something in my ear telling me to turn around.

Unable to gain entrance into the laundry room, I ended up meeting her in the media room in the library. There wasn't anybody at the library but an old head reading the paper. I searched for Officer Lopez but I soon found her sitting near the magazines and newspapers.

I took a seat next to her and requested for the work. She pulled out a Zip Lock bag of cocaine and handed to me under the table. I used the rubber band that had the bag wrapped up to tie around my penis.

She scooted over and gave me a passionate kiss on my lips. She told me that this would be the last time that she will do this for me. Officer Lopez continued to explain her reasoning and I truly understood. I wasn't tripping because I was going home in two months.

Boom!

A loud bang came from behind me. Both of us almost jumped out of our seats from the noise. We turned towards the direction from which the noise came from and my heart skipped a beat. I looked back at Officer Lopez and she remained in shock.

Officer Thurman busted into the library with multiple guards with him. They were armed to the "T" with guns and combat gear. Another guard had a dog on a leash. Officer Thurman wore this grimace look on his face as he continued to step closer to us. I knew he had set us up.

"Put your hands behind your back," an officer said with his gun aimed on me.

I wanted to dig down in my pants and pull this ounce of coke from my penis but I didn't want to give them any reasons to do me like they did my brother Christian. I did what I was told and slowly put my hands around my back.

With the cold metal wrapped around my wrist, Officer Thurman leaned over and whispered in my ear, "I told you to cut me in. That bitch don't have pull like me."

"Reese, I didn't mean to get you in this mess," Officer Lopez cried.

The look on her face was of disbelief. I knew that she didn't have anything to do with it but damn. I should have went with my instincts and said fuck this petty ass shit.

The outside judge sentenced me to additional seven years to my sentence without the chance of parole. I had to serve out another bid. The news was devastating to Diana and my son. They had high hopes of me coming home but now those hopes are gone. I looked in my son's eyes and realized that the next time I would be able to hold him again he would almost be a grown man. I could only pray that the love Diana had for me was everlasting. This was another blow to our union.

Chapter 18

Diana

I checked the time on my cell phone, then over to Rico, we were both excited to receive a call from his daddy. Rico sat watching ESPN on the couch with his long legs stretched out. Rico grew to be 6'5 and a little over 200 pounds. He was chomping on a bowl of fruit and drinking Gatorade in front of the 90 inch flat screen. He was just like his father on that aspect. Rico sat in front of the TV waiting for the sportscasters to mention his team and hopefully his name. Rico was highly recruited although he was only a junior in high school. Rico had his mine set on going to school at the University of Dayton because he wanted his dad to be able to attend every game. I wanted him to go to Ohio State but he had his mind set. His team had won 32 straight games and tonight they were to fight for a state title. Rico remained humble and believed that he had to study the ESPN highlights for some new moves if his team were to win. He knew that the coach on the other bench would know each one of his moves and would come prepared.

Since a kid Rico knew what his father and I did for a living but he didn't find any interest. He really didn't like the whole street life thing and was deep into his books and sports. He watched everyone one around me get sucked into the game and their whole life had changed. I was a proud mother of a smart kid.

Reese would beg for me to write down his game stats after games so that he could brag to his fellow inmates about his son. I found it to be irritating at times but I did everything in my power to make sure that everyone was happy. Reese had been living through Rico these last two years. I honestly believed that Rico saved his father from himself. Reese could have went into that prison and hustled in there also but he thought about Rico. I saw it in his face when we go see him on holidays and it read true disgust of himself.

Reese finally called and gave me careful instruction to where and how he wanted me to pick him up. Reese wanted out of that place so bad that he didn't want any assistance from the government and wanted me to pick him up personally. The prison was in Indiana. Reese had been moved from the FCI in Kentucky after his security level was raised from the added charges he had occurred. Reese wanted me to drive out there, pick him up and go out to eat. When I asked what he wanted he mentioned some Popeye's. He had spent 13 years of his life behind bars and he wanted chicken. Out of all of the restaurants he could have mentioned he asked for Popeye's chicken. He said he was feenin' for some good chicken. I laughed.

Before I passed the phone to over to Rico, I asked Reese what size he believes he's in now. Reese had sculpted his body perfectly. His pectoral muscles got huge along with his arms. I'd often dreamed of just lying on his chest, rubbing my hands over his chest down his ripped abs. I believed I was more excited about him coming home more than anyone. Reese gave me his sizes and I wrote them down. I already had planned on getting his clothes now before I had to handle business.

I passed the phone to Rico who was patiently waiting to speak to him. I rushed to my room to get my purse to go shopping for my man.

Rico and Reese didn't have much in common with each other but they had sports. They would sit and talk on the phone before each game. They made that a tradition. Tonight Rico promised to get his father a triple double and at the end of the game give the whole city a shout-out on television.

Rico wanted me to attend his high school basketball game tonight but I had to meet Juan people tonight in Cincinnati and Rico's game was in Columbus. Rico was wanting me to go bad because he wanted to celebrate cutting down the nets with me. He told me that all of his ideals celebrated their championships with their families and he wanted to also. I told him that he would have plenty of opportunities to celebrate with me. I imagined with him bringing me to his championship NBA game.

Rico ended his call with his father and was pumped up for the game. I had to break the news to Rico about me not being able to attend the game. I had to drive to Cincinnati at the same location when we first met to pick up the package. Juan and I planned this last month before the state tournament was in full effect. Juan was delivering it personally and was going to chill out there anticipating to meet his friend now on the other side of the wall. He said that he was throwing in a few extra bricks to celebrate. This man had cake for real.

B called me ready to meet with Juan but I had to calm him down with the news of me shopping. B said he was up for the challenge.

Three hours of shopping in these heels had my feet killing me. I was glad that I brought B along with me. B had expensive taste but it was well worth it for my husband. We had one last place to go and that was the shoe store. I bought Reese every new shoe that recently came out. I looked for B to assist me with the bags and I noticed him out in the hallway talking to an attractive woman. Her faced was familiar.

Sky.

I went against my original thought of leaving B but time was ticking. I had things to do and people to see.

B saw me coming a mile away. He continued to talk but he wore this weird look on his face. I knew who the chic was. Men be so extra. I was not about to cause a seen in a crowded mall for no damn reason.

"Hello," I politely said.

"Hi," Sky answered, giving me the respect that I deserved.

"I don't mean to be rude by interrupting y'all conversation but B we have to go."

"Oh it's okay," she had replied.

"Give me a five little man," B said reaching around Sky's big butt.

I didn't even notice the young boy sitting on the wooded bench behind her. He had locks of hair and wore a familiar beautiful smile. I knew he couldn't be more than six or so. I gave the little man a wave and shot him a friendly smile back.

"That's your son?" I asked Sky.

She turned around to look at him. B was playing with him like he use to with Rico. I thought it was cute to see his softer side from time to time. B was always a hard ass.

"Yes, that's my boy."

"He's beautiful," I said taking a closer step to look at him.

"It was nice to see you again. You have my number don't lose it," B said trying to sound smooth.

When we pulled up in front of my house, B climbed out and grabbed the duffle bag full of product. He was excited to get to work. He wanted five bricks just for himself but I planned on giving Reese everything and washing my hands from the job. My days of hustling were over. I didn't understand how Reese could do this. I have missed so much time away from Rico that I was questioned a lot by his friends who I was. It was embarrassing.

We entered into the house and I sat my phone down on the coffee table. I checked the time and figured that I could get some sleep in before I jumped on the interstate. B started to inspect a brick but I stopped him in his tracks. I told him that the dope was spoken for. He already knew who I was talking about. He waited a second to allow my words to sink in then he had went off.

I stood a few feet away from this clown our family called friend. Hearing him bringing up Sky and the thought of her son being Rico's brother had me on fire. He wanted me to believe that Reese got that chic pregnant while he was locked up in a federal institution. I wanted to hit his ass with a frying pan or something. B continued to cuss at me but I ignored his ass. I wasn't going to allow him to ruin my night. Besides, I had to pick up my man in a few hours.

"Bitch, are you listening to me?" B shouted stepping closer.

"B you need to take your ass up and out of my house."

"I am sitting here telling your husband ain't shit but a liar and you are just going to play me to the left like that? You saw the boy and he looked just like Reese and you know it."

"B move! Don't touch me man! I trusted you as a friend."

"A friend?"

"What else are we?"

160

"Diana don't act like that. Now I can't touch you? Girl you must be crazy."

"No you can't!" I snapped pulling away from his grasp.

"Diana now you are on some new shit. Like we didn't fuck before," B smiled.

"B, I was drunk and taking medicine for depression. I was going through a lot then. You had basically raped me fool. I didn't know what I was doing and I still don't."

"Yeah whatever. You remembered that shit."

"Can you please leave?"

"What are you going to do? Are you going to call the police with a duffle bag full of bricks on your dining table."

"You are a mess."

"Listen here. How about we go up to the room make up and shit I will even drive you to pick Reese up in the morning."

"You ain't shit. Is this how you treat your so called best friend?"

"Best friend. That muthafucka ain't no friend of mine! A friend won't leave his boy on the street all fucked up!" B said biting his lip.

"You are not wanting for anything. You have several cars, a house, and look at the clothes on your back. Reese did that," I pointed at him.

"No we did that! Reese ain't did shit for me!"

"You are tripping. I believe it's time for you to go."

"I will leave after you give me what I want. You are not going to play me now because Reese is coming home."

Not paying attention to anything he had to say, I stepped rapidly to the kitchen doors. Soon as I turned my back to open the French doors that led out to the back yard, B grabbed me from the back putting his manhood all on me. He creeped me out with the thought of him touching me. I tried to wiggle myself out of his grasp but it seemed like the more I moved the tighter he hugged me. Not able to move my arms or grab something in the kitchen, I had to think quickly. With my heel of my shoe I stepped as hard as I could on his foot. I must have found a toe. He let out a scream and backed up. I knew that he was going to try to hit me so I rushed over to my knives and grabbed the first one I gotten my hands on.

"B leave me alone and get the hell out of my house!" I demanded.

"Bitch you are pulling out knives now," he giggled.

"Yes I am. And I will use the muthafucka on your ass also!"

"You better put it down before somebody get hurt."

"B just get the fuck out of my house!"

B ran like he was being chased by the police towards me. He tackled me to the floor and slapped me hard to the face. He shouted about giving him some pussy but I was planning on giving him a knife to his throat. I tried kneeing him in the balls but it didn't work. I searched frantically for the knife but it wasn't in sight. B shouted again then punched me like a man. I shouted for the neighbors to call the police. He punched me harder. My eyes saw nothing but darkness for a second. I felt him tugging at my pants to pull them off. He shouted for me to stop moving but I squirmed and flopped like a fish out of water. I reached for his face and tried to scratch him but he already was aware and sat on top of me and delivered more blows.

I must have been unconscious for a few minutes because when I woke up he wasn't anywhere in sight. I was scared to feel if I had my pants on and luckily I did. I didn't even stand up before I started praying and thanking God that this man didn't rap me. I rolled over on my side to get some leverage and I noticed a puddle of blood on the floor. My hair had blood drench in it. I began to touch my face knowing it was marked with lumps and bruises. Finally I found the knife and it was also covered with blood.

Using the kitchen island I pulled myself up to my feet. I only had one heel on so I kicked it to the side. Sluggishly I managed to walk towards the living room couch. I was feeling exhausted. Each step felt as if I was walking in deep water. All I could hear was the beating of my heart. The beating seemed to start to slow down. I saw my phone on the coffee table and with everything in me I reached for it. I feel down to the floor unable to move a muscle. The glass from the coffee table didn't seem to faze me. My heart gave up and I took my last breath looking at the pictures of Reese holding Rico when he was born.

Epilogue

Rico

My friend's parents parked their car next to my mother's in the driveway. They congratulated me and waited for me to hop out. I grabbed my bag of equipment and the Ohio medallion to show to my mom. I know that she would be proud. My mom had a room in the house specifically for my trophies, awards and jerseys that I wore over the years. She claimed that she was keeping all of this stuff for my father to see but I knew better. My mom bragged about me on a daily. I was anticipating to hear her excitement. Although she didn't make it I understood what she had to do. I didn't think that she would have beat me home knowing how long she was usually out all night. I was happy to see her home so I rushed for the door to surprise her with the medallion. My mom was my number one fan and true supporter. When I won, I felt like I won for her. She had sacrificed so much for me and I planned on repaying her when I finally made it. I didn't want either of my parents thinking about the dope game after I signed my first check.

With the key in the door I turned the knob to open. Suddenly I felt a cold draft of air hit me in the face after I had closed the door.

"Mom! Where are you? I have something to show you," I shouted stepping away from the foyer.

I wondered if she was lying in her bed getting some rest before she went to pick my dad up from prison. She was usually a night-owl staying up at the wee hours of the morning. I dropped my bag at the door and proceed for her room.

My feet stopped moving when I saw my mother sprawled out over the floor. My throat became dry as I tried to call out for her. She wasn't moving. It looked bad. I wondered if she slipped on something and feel onto the table. Glass was all over the carpet. I reached down to pick her up but her arm was covered with blood. I knew that she was gone from this life. I pulled out my cell phone to call the ambulance, then again I felt the cold draft. I walked towards the draft and noticed the kitchen door was wide open.

The closer I inched towards the kitchen I saw more and more blood. The kitchen island had a hand print with blood. I stepped closer, the tile floor was covered with blood. The floor had so much blood that a regular mop couldn't clean it up. This had to be professionally cleaned.

Damn! Somebody broke in and killed my mother. I knew that whoever that did this was acting because of drugs. Drugs did crazy things to a person mind if they were a fiend and even worst things if they were in the game. I was going to find out who did this no matter what. I wanted someone to pay immediately. I rushed to my mother's bedroom and looked for her gun. She normally kept her gun next to her in her nightstand. Nothing was in

166

there but a few things that I wished I didn't see. Before rushing out of her room I checked one more spot. I looked in her closet and found a brand new handgun with ammo. I tucked the gun in my warmup pants and went back to the living room.

The emergency operator said that they were sending a patrol car and emergency squad. I sat on the couch looking at my mother's lifeless body. I didn't understand how could life be so damn hard. I felt like everything and everyone that I loved had been taken from me. How was I going to live without the person that I lived for.

The sirens became closer. I cried like a baby with the thought of losing my mother forever. I felt like I had to do something or go somewhere. I searched the room with my eyes for my mother's car keys. The keys were right next to her body. I noticed a black duffle bag on the side of the loveseat. I quickly opened the bag and looked inside. I found bricks of what I assumed was drugs. I zipped the bag up and hurried for her car. I threw the bag on the floor and pulled off. The police arrived right out front of the house just seconds after I pulled off.

My mind raced with so many thoughts. I wanted to go home but I couldn't be in a house that took my mother from me. I decided to call Uncle B. I knew that he would find out whomever took my mother's life.

Uncle B met me not too far from the house. His car was clean. No literally like he had just had it detailed. His car was nice and it made my friends wonder when B would come to school in this ride. He was driving an old school Monte Carlo.

I climbed into his car and closed the door behind me. His car smelled like weed mixed with a lavender scent. We shook hands and I noticed a scratch on his arm. My eyes examined his face and hands. B must have noticed me checking him out. He said that he just left a girl's house and they were having some rough sex. B laughed and I joined in. He said he left her to come out and get something to eat, then he was headed home.

I told him what I saw at the house and he sounded as if he was about to cry himself. I never heard him in this state. B started asking me questions about the house and what my mother might have died from. I tried to remember her lifeless body and remembered seeing cuts over her body. He said that he would find out who killed her and have them dealt with.

Ending our conversation, I began to climb out of the car. He stopped me asking if there was anything else that he could help me with.

"I found a bag?"

"A bag?" He asked looking at me confused.

"Yeah, I found a bag filled with dope?" I answered.

B stared out of the windshield. His right hand firmly gripped the stirring wheel.

"I don't know what to do with it."

"Shit you don't know what to do with it. Well, let Uncle B show you."

A LETTER TO MY READERS

I want every one of my readers to know that I appreciate y'all and your continued support for all of my titles. This series wouldn't be such a success without you all. My books Escaping The Allure Of The Game 1-3, I Don't Trust You, and The Streets Call Me Treasure have been flooding the streets like crazy. I enjoy your reviews and meeting you all at book events. I promise to continue to bring that heat with more titles to come.

Thank you for the love and support.

Yours Truly,

Shaunta Kenerly

Mr. Paperback

www.ingramcontent.com/pod-product-compliance
Lightning Source LLC
Chambersburg PA
CBHW061722020426
42331CB00006B/1054